ISBN 978-1-331-06444-2
PIBN 10140146

Introduction

Of Canonical and Non-Canonical Books

(i.) He who takes up this booklet and sees it styled 'Apocryphal' will doubtless wonder why one dubs it with so sinister a name. For this says just about the same as 'furtive,' 'disguised,' not to say 'thievish' or 'sneaking.' But, alas, we have all been taught to feel a little qualm when we buy a Bible that contains the Apocrypha, lest we be entering among bad companions, or at least are encouraging booksellers in bringing too near to very precious pages some others that are verily profane.

Yet, let us pause to reflect what 'Canonical' means to us, and while our Creeds and our Greek warn us that 'the Canon is our Rule of Faith and Practice,' very few do look to canonical books to find either. Neither one sort of men among us nor another studies Leviticus for such ends, although, verily, it was meant as a stern rule of both Faith and Practice in its time; and even Romans has scarcely ever been counted as practically canonical in such sense. The words 'Canonical' and 'Apocryphal' have practically been always and purely esthetic distinctions.

(ii.) Serious it is, however, to find that by calling Esdras I. and II. uncanonical and apocryphal, we have accustomed ourselves to think little or lightly, or even not at all, of a great part of the life of our Lord Jesus. Herein we have really hurt Him and our own souls. This present little volume hopes to heal these wounds somewhat.

For consider how a knowledge of Jesus and of His Words and Love and Death depends on a knowledge of the people who lived round about Him, and on a knowledge of the nationality He shared with them. To know Jesus depends on knowing the Jew, despised though he has been. Therein the Jew has been singularly like Jesus, writ large, for each has been, and is, a marvellous microcosm, ay, and macrocosm of real life; each has been 'rejected of men,' and each also 'sees his seed and prolongs his days.' That grows plain to the reader of Esdras I. and II.

For who shall know the Jewish nationality who does not feel the fight of the books of Maccabees? Who shall understand the Lord's yearning to convince or to condemn, to soothe or smite the Pharisee dissenter if he does not feel the wail of the Psalms of Solomon? Who shall see the justice of Jesus towards a Nicodemus if he have not sat with Jesus among the thinkers and writers and readers of 'Wisdom'? Or who shall sit beneath the Cross and drop hot tears on that pitiful spot realising that the Paschal Lamb of God feeds his soul, if he turns careless away from the hunger to eat the Passover that moves in every word of Esdras I.? As for Esdras II., read his agony and his faith, and understand why Jesus said, 'Thou art not far from the Kingdom of God.'

(iii.) These two little pamphlets might well be called canonical and normative for him who would preach Christ. For to know them and their origin and their doctrine and their significance is to know the souls whom Jesus tried to heal and help, and to whose hunger for a 'Christ' and for a 'Saviour' He cried, 'Come unto Me.' It was to their agony over inborn sin and to their longing for a new heaven and a new earth that Paul and John preached. Here in Esdras I. and II. is canon for a teacher of Christianity.

Of the Christian's Need for Esdras I. and II.

(i.) Let us condescend to a few particulars. Of late a true and fine instinct has said that we to-day must know more of the 'Historical Christ.' We feel that we must see and touch the Jesus of actual events in Nazareth, and as He lived in that first century. We think that if we should see Him and come to Him we should find true rest, and more rest, for our souls. Good; come near and look.

We shall find Him, a young man, sitting often amid a dervish-like company. For twenty years one of such a company was surely Joseph, and Mary was never far from his side. You may almost hear one of these same dervishes reciting aloud paragraphs of Esdras I. Perhaps it is his own soul's writing. The booklet is the breath of Jesus's environment.

(ii.) Recall that strong yet sacred sentence in John i. that makes us tremble still, and always makes us glad :—

'The Word became Flesh.'

The utterance of God in and through flesh, and men, and the human race goes on ever, as surely as God ever lives and must speak forever. But knowing all that, we still seek something more, something more pointedly defined. 'We would see Jesus!' And we would see how *He became*. We would know how His very body took form, how features in Him fashioned themselves, how thought-seeds sank into His mind, and sprang to possessions and to parts of the very Man of God. What was wont to kindle His eye, to redden His cheek and brow with eagerness? What were His ways? To answer this yearning no merely imagined pictures will suffice. We shall turn unfilled from them, although such imaginations of our hearts be woven of traits and threads that we have seen and loved in noble souls of our own day. Some of these present-day features may indeed date from long ago; but some come from the experiences, customs, philosophies of the Evangelical Revival or of the Puritans, or of the Reformers, or of the great time of Renascence, or from the Middle Ages or Darker Days before. All are precious, and all are features of the Body of Christ Living on Forever: but they are still not features that He bore in His days on earth. Subjective fancying of what Jesus was may be poetry, and is often very beautiful and valuable; but it is not the Jesus of the Gospels. For knowledge of that we shall get light from Esdras I. and II.

(iii.) Nor may we follow the tempting plan of piecing together, as in a puzzle, all the various records written and handed down concerning Jesus in our New Testament. If we do, we shall then have to say in one breath that He both did say or do, and also did not say or do, this and that. All records are precious material for history and a historical picture of Jesus or of any other soul; and so each jot or tittle must be strictly and lovingly weighed and accorded its exactly due influence in developing our great portrait. But so, also, no prejudice must dare to bar any word, or line, or opinion held anywhere in those days. Some singular contributions are to be got from Esdras I. and II., for these were written in and about the very days of Jesus. It will not do to think that traditionally canonical scriptures only may furnish us with material for such a sacred task. History knows no canon save its own events, and it reads every possible record to find these.

(iv.) The historical portraiture of Jesus must include the background against which He stands, the arena where He lived and loved and saved. Our knowledge of Him is always felt to depend on the words and mind of those men who had been with Him. He was just the *vis viva* that made them be what they were; and we study the *vis viva* by observing the phenomena it produces. We see Jesus by seeing Paul and the twelve and many another. But how shall we know what He made them unless we know what they were before the light of His face and love and voice fell on them? Now, the heart and the hopes, the hunger, the agonies, the joys and the griefs—in short, the men whom Jesus changed are to be seen before their change in Esdras I., and especially in Esdras II.

(v.) When we look closely at those men, the unchanged men, as they live and think and speak in these two little pamphlets, we can see how their souls grew to be what they were. We seem to hear them cry out, with a strange pathos, the need and nature of their souls. They say, 'We are not one or two; we are a great company and congregation of weary souls, that speak often one to another, and say unto our God, "How long, O Lord." Among us are children and fathers and fathers' fathers, and we are all labouring and heavy-laden. We believe that God will help us. We do and say and observe those things and ways and words that we hope will please Him. He has revealed, He does reveal, He will reveal His mind ever more and more to us.

O, when will He show us His kingdom?' We wonder as we read. We see that Jesus brought just what these souls needed. He gave them power to rest in God. But, as we listen to their cry, we are forced to ask how they came to attain so high a height. What were the generation that had begotten such high hope and grasp, hunger and vision? As we feel the compulsion to this question, there steals in upon us the understanding that to know the source whence these came is to know the source whence Jesus came Himself.

(vi.) Let us think of it that Christians of those days saw and said, 'Jesus was Himself of this people, the Jews, according to the flesh.' There is a customary opinion that we need not know Joseph: what Joseph was has nothing to do with what our Lord Jesus was. Yet we must know the father of Mary. He cannot be left out, nor may her fathers' fathers be passed by. Of them Jesus was according to the flesh. So shall we know the story of Mary's soul, and of the matrons and the maidens who sat with her behind the screens of the synagogues. So shall we know the boys and girls whom those told at home about Moses and the Prophets and all the Writings they had been hearing read. So shall we know the schoolboy days of Jesus, and the play times and the comrades of those years. Quite possibly some of these comrades helped to write Esdras I., say A.D. 20; and quite surely some of them helped to mould the younger life of the writer of Esdras II., say A.D. 90.

What pictures rose before those lads as the rabbi schoolmasters told of the dear, dear past; and as together they chanted daily the Hymns and Psalms sung or written by Pharisee dissenters or by stately official Sadducees. How did these boys' eyes wonder together at the words:—

> 'Whom have I in heaven but Thee:
> None upon earth do I desire beside Thee!'

Did their pulses beat slow at the awful cruelty of the lines:—

> 'Happy shall he be, that taketh and dasheth thy little ones
> Against the rock!'

To study Jesus thus has not been our wont; but it is our duty. We have been leaving out of our ken visions of Him which we may see clearly in these Jewish comrades of His. Does anyone fear that this may make us think less of Him? Will it make us wonder whether there was left any good and godlike thing for Him to bring? Nay, then it will be enough to read Esdras II. alongside of Romans vii. It will be enough to remember how He told them they were not far from the Kingdom, and that when the best of them, directly or indirectly, murdered Him, He prayed, 'Father, forgive them, for they know not what they do.' He brought!—what? He brought Himself; and the sight of that, the knowledge of Him, was power enough to win them to oneness with Him. It did prove to be enough to create many into His likeness.

(vii.) Let us look back, however, more intently. It was the faith of the devout and beautiful men among us not long ago that Malachi closed, say 500 B.C., all the utterances of God to men that were ever given before Jesus came. Indeed, it was even pointed out that the last words of Malachi were, 'Lest I come and smite the earth with a curse!' Men might well be in dread after that, lest any other words of such an Awful Spirit should be uttered to them. God was actually conceived, by our fellows a generation ago, as having sat silent in the heavens for five hundred years. So long had the poor souls of earth had no ear nor heart for voices from the Unseen, the Eternal, the Almighty!

The theory was pathetic. Thank God, it was to flee away before the eyes of the student, like darkness from the face of the dawn. All may now read the wonderful exuberance of literature which that young Judaism—thoughtful, keen, reverent, advancing with a marvellous spirit of progress—produced in those very same five centuries. Intensely devoted the people of this new religion were, determined to get and give knowledge of their God, for themselves and for all peoples. They set in their innermost shrine, beneath the Mercy Seat, the words:—

'Here will our God ever come to reveal to us more and more of His Mind.'

The purpose of all God's Providence seemed to them clearly to be this, 'that all nations might know the character of their God Iahweh.' They had, indeed, learned that faith from their Hebrew prophet-fathers; but they searched out and exalted their old faiths, editing with many a comment the words of prophets, of narrators, and of poets. They came together in trysted assemblies, and in synagogues all over the world wherever they might be dwelling, to confer, to argue, to murmur aloud their faith, to tell it to their children and to the strangers, so that all might learn that wisdom which begins, and has its heart, and finds its crown, in the fear of the Lord Iahweh. They wrote new settings of His deeds in the past; they chanted hallelujahs before Him with many a stirring accompaniment; they preached in the days of darkness that often came, counting hope for the future the best sermon for the present. Thus did they compose constantly new enlargements of their Divine Torah, *i.e.*, doctrine, and ever new books of Psalms, and ever richer volumes of

Wisdom, and cunning paragraphs of Haggada, *i.e.*, enriching expositions. Above all, they dreamed new and always newer Apocalypses, or Revelations, concerning the ways that their God would take for the establishment of righteousness in the times to come. Such was young Judaism; such its faiths, and such its literary diligence, and its keen mental activities.

Among the more ordinary readers, the last-named class of writings, the Apocalypses, found chief favour in hours when oppressions came; and, of all their Apocalypses, that which in this volume we call the Second Book of Esdras was perhaps the finest. For times of less trouble, the simpler souls loved bright stories glorifying the past; and the First Book of Esdras is an excellent example of such works. Perhaps reading these will help us to a more worthy estimate of the Jews than has been customary.

The Particular Origin of Esdras I.

(i.) Above, once and again, it has been said that our two little pamphlets were fruits of a great history. Naturally a history that could culminate in 'Jesus according to the flesh' must have been full of great impulses towards development, threaded by great life-lines, and moved by an unconquerable vitality. We have to try to realise and see somewhat of those impulses, and life-lines and that vitality.

(ii.) Our booklets are essentially Jewish in the sense that the religion, thought and observances which they represent are not properly to be counted Hebrew. Judaism was not the still higher development of what Hebraism had attained when the

Exile overthrew it, about 600 B.C. The outburst of the prophesyings in the eighth century concerning Iahweh as a God of Goodness had been followed within a hundred years by a notable success. The little nation accepted in 620 B.C. a new charter system of government and religion, based, as it seemed, on the principles which those prophets had preached. But within a generation another prophet, Jeremiah, pointed out that the new methods were hollow : real life with God must be something far deeper. Here, now, was a great dividing of the ways; and our two pamphlets in this volume are in some sense fruits of the twin branches.

(iii.) Jeremiah led Hebraism away up towards its highest climax, as we see it in the Four Lyrics of Isaiah xlii., xlix., l. and liii. These show the climax of Hebraism as a thoughtfulness concerning the Unseen, concerning Suffering, concerning Sin, and concerning the Conquest of Evil. In Esdras II. we shall see late Judaism of Jesus's time rising again towards this same height.

(iv.) But the other line of the fork was followed by Ezekiel in his visions in Babylon. To him, and in the opinion of his school, God must be far away from minds that are thoughtful while simple : only upon esthetic form, display, ceremonial, etiquette, ritual, and on a spirit that loves this will Deity smile. In Esdras I. we shall see a Jew of Jesus's time who holds that faith.

(v.) But which was to prevail first, among the poor remnant left in Judæa, and gradually restoring itself to health and shapeliness? The latter character was sure to do so among these feeble folk ; at first, and for many a day until the inner vitality that God ever makes and means in men's souls should of living necessity grow and burst its forms, grow again, and become ever richer, deeper, truer.

Ere two centuries passed from the beginning of Exile, about 400 B.C., the new feeble Jewish folk had grown enough to desire and to adopt a fresh charter, a new fabric as the esthetic garb that would please God. The fine details of it can be read in that contributory document or element in the Old Testament story, which scholars have discovered for us and which they call the 'Priestly Book,' beginning in Genesis i. and running on, especially visible in Exodus and Leviticus, and continuing to the end of Kings. Now our reader will begin to see how we trace the marks of the far-off coming of the First Book of Esdras.

(vi.) For let us recall the notable and even startling feature of that Priestly Charter, or Aaronite system, and its hierarchy, and sanctuary. We have said already that in the very sacredest centre of it all was the recorded expectation of growth, enlargement, addition in opinions and customs. Iahweh would sit in the Holiest Place, to give to a Representative Man ever new revelations.

No wonder, then, that this Priestly Document itself grew larger and larger, was touched and built up by fresh words, passages, institutions and methods. Then it was enlarged far more by interweaving with it other and older precious traditions and records of similar things, and times, and persons, and theologies; until it shows new stratifications and an imbedded picture of its own story and growth as rich as the geological depths we stand upon.

(vii.) At last, advance went so far that an entirely new view of the whole story of the past seemed necessary in the eyes of an enthusiastic scribe. He wrote down such, beginning at the creation with the words 'Adam, Seth, Enosh,' and ending with the Jewish affairs of the days of Alexander the Great, say 300 B.C. This new book we call 'Chronicles.' No wonder that it was at first suspected. It was allowed into the Sacred Collection of Writings only very late, and even then was made to stand last in that collection.

Yet not altogether so: long before 'Chronicles' was admitted, it was observed that the concluding parts of the same told a story of matters after the Exile which was not already contained elsewhere in the collection. For 'Kings' had ended when the Exile began. The concluding parts were therefore torn off, somewhat roughly indeed, as the student easily sees; and these fragments were set within the collection under the names 'Ezra' and 'Nehemiah.' They were followed at some later day by the truncated 'Chronicles,' when the suspicion of illegitimacy had grown feeble. Our Esdras I. is simply an effort of a Greek Jew with a missionary spirit who thought to keep his scattered fellow Jews acquainted in some fashion with the story of the past, and therefore wrote 'Ezra' in Greek.

(viii.) But let us draw nearer to that missionary, who wrote Esdras I. Life and godliness in Judæa, and among scattered Jews, needed far more than a ceremonial worship, by a few persons, in one Temple, in one city. All would have become atheists if that plan had been everything to them. It had been the 'saving plan' of the old Deuteronomists of Josiah's time, but its impossibilities compelled men to find some other ways of communion with the Unseen. For commune with God they would, and they must and they did. Therefore they met in all places where they settled; and, calling their meeting places 'synagogues,' they held devotional services. They sang and they prayed; but especially they bid someone read aloud the Hebrew scriptures. Then for the sake of the many who had ceased to understand Hebrew there would stand up the interpreter, who 'gave the sense'; or, to use Eastern words, they had a 'dragom-an' who gave 'targum,' 'dragom,' *i.e.*, 'version,' in the vernacular. Our Esdras I. is a 'version' or 'targum' in the vernacular Greek of a land, Palestine, Egypt, or elsewhere, where Greek was spoken.

(ix.) We may come nearer still. Those interpreters were preachers, and sought to expound the faith of the texts they read, as they believed they saw it there. Ay, they had faith, as strong as that of any preachers ever since, that their souls were called of God to their task, and that they were moved of Him, when they felt eager to preach the thoughts that burned within them. They had been told by their great Priestly Charter that God had more light and truth to shed forth from His Spirit. They believed that all new things which they felt to be good things were revealed to them by Him. So they enlarged and 'read in' their subjective views, making 'Exposition,' or as they called it 'Haggada,' even to subtractions and additions and alterations, without any hesitation. Absolutely the opposite was this from what we might to-day call a 'falsification' or 'perversion.' What they read in, or read out, or read differently, was what they firmly believed their God had bidden them so read.

So their writings became verily records of their own souls, their own conceptions, their own ways of thinking and customs of worship, a record indeed of their own lives and their own times, and far less a record of the conceptions and times of the past. Thus Esdras I. is a picture of the mind of a man who lived contemporaneously with Jesus, and may have heard Him preach. Even although he wrote Greek and knew it fairly well, he may have lived in Palestine and in Galilee; as did Josephus, who knew the book, and used it, and copied much of it into his own works.

THE ORIGIN OF ESDRAS II.

(i.) The spirit of some simple souls that listened to those versions was inspired to go much farther. The Maccabean books tell us a little of one side of the bitter experiences and also the enthusiastic hopes shared by those Jews a century and a half before Jesus's birth. A brilliant but wayward Greek prince of Syria, having 'suzerainty' over Jewry, thought it was time to force all Jews to be altogether Greek.

The primary outcome of that brilliant madness was the organisation for defence that Judas Maccabeus and his father and brothers led. They were grandly victorious. The organisation with which they conquered became the new, independent, Maccabean or Hasmonæan Jewish state. Presently the grateful people cried to Simon, the fourth of these leaders:—

> 'Be thou and thy sons henceforth forever our Royal House:
> 'And be thou and thy heirs henceforward our High Priests.'

This was in 141 B.C. We need not describe the despair of other guidance, royal or priestly, that forced that election from the breathless folk. But while the books of the Maccabees and the Sadducee Psalms, ii. and cx. in our Psalm Book, glorify this choice and elevation, the deed was illegitimate in the eyes of the Devoted, the lovers of the Davidic dynasty and of the

Aaronic hierarchy. Dissent rose in stern earnest. The dissenters were dubbed 'Pharisi,' *i.e.*, 'Dissenting' men; and the loyalists were called 'Zadoki,' 'Sadducee' men, because once long ago, as story told, David had made parallel change, when he discarded the 'Eli' line of priests and put Zadok and his house into the court pontificate. Here we find the beginning of that bitter antagonism of Jesus's times, of which Esdras II. gives illustration.

More particularly, however, the story is that while in their bitterness the dissenters grew full of hatreds they were even more filled with hopes of coming restoration of the real Rule of God, under the sceptre of a true Son of Man, who should receive the Unseen Anointing and become God's own representative 'Mashiah' or Christ. Here is one of the kernel tenets of the faith of Esdras II. In many ways, and out of the pain and sense of sin and wrong on every hand, the expectations of these dissenting souls hungered for deliverance to come; until out of very fastings and tears and agony of prayer were conceived those visions of 'the age that should come' which we read in 'Daniel,' in 'Enoch,' in 'John'; and more nobly uttered than in any of these we read them in the Revelation or Apocalypse of Esdras II. This dropped in rhapsody from the lips and pen of a contemporary of our Lord perhaps, more certainly a contemporary of Paul and of John the Evangelist.

(ii.) Such writers ascribed their ideas to 'Ezra,' or to 'Enoch,' or to 'Daniel,' and to other great ancestors. For they came easily to the fancy that those old heroes had had such visions; and when the title 'Ezra' or 'Esdras' was put at the head of the composition, it was set there in perfect honesty, and out of conviction that this was the will of the great Spirit. To Him they ascribed all their own subjective dreams, thoughts, and opinions, just as much as the events going on around them.

There was indeed one feature of the times which in a sense forced these apocalyptists to conceal their own authorship. This is well described by Gunkel in his work on Esdras II. It is this, that there arose then, as in all times, a tendency to exalt some traditionally important ancestral persons and to canonise certain names, such as Moses, David, Isaiah, Daniel, Ezra. In exactly the same measure it was difficult for any new writer, even such as had great ability, to command a hearing. This may help to explain even why we possess no writing of Jesus, whether He ever composed such or not. But a writer eager to tell men his thoughts, and perhaps not gifted with much oral eloquence, would be driven by this very difficulty to fancy that what he thought must have been thought before by the greatest souls of his race. He would therefore unhesitatingly lay his writings on the knees of anyone whom he counted his great hero. And he would firmly believe that this course was taught to him by the Divine guiding Spirit, and was most natural, worthy and righteous. Such then were many thinkers and writers among the contemporaries of our Lord. Such was the society among whom He was brought to birth and moulded, in home, in school and in all the affairs of life. By understanding these men through such literature we understand Him, His work, His word, His love and His healing of souls and all life. We do well, therefore, to read Esdras I. and II.

# of Esdras

ANALYSIS OF THE CONTENTS OF ESDRAS I.

(i.) At once the student will discover that there are many forms in which this little pamphlet has come down from long ago to us. These are all to be found enumerated in the Bible Dictionaries and Encyclopaedias, and in the critical Text Studies by specialists concerning the Greek Bible called the Septuagint. Among the most valuable of the latter are the works of Swete in English and of de Lagarde in German. To illustrate this variety sufficiently for present aims and space, we give in the Notes at the end of this volume some account of various passages, verses, words, etc., to be found in the so-called 'Lucian' text of the Greek Bible, as these vary from the 'Revised Version' which we print.

The 'Lucian' text was the ecclesiastically authoritative form used in the churches of the Provinces of Antioch and Constantinople in the days of the scholar and martyr Lucian, who wrote it out in a careful scholarly sort about 300 A.D. This text has been edited for us by the late Professor Paul de Lagarde.

The text printed in the body of our volume is that given in the old 'Authorised Version.' The authors of the Revised Version of 1895-1896 claim for their product simply correctness of translation from the currently accessible Greek. They announce distinctly in their preface that the Greek they translate is not a 'critical' text; it is not the result of careful study concerning the history of the book. Such a critical text of this or any part of the Greek Bible has not yet been prepared, although work is steadily proceeding towards that much desired end.

(ii.) In any case this 'First Book of Esdras' is one of several parallel efforts to tell Greek readers of our Lord's time something, little or much, old or new, concerning the 'Ezra,' who is described in the bilingual book—partly Hebrew and partly Aramaic or Syriac—of that name in the Old Testament. We have shown how the Greek version-makers wove their own ideas and the habits of thought and worship of their own times into the versions they made. Quite regardless were they whether the original Hebrew and Aramaic authors had known these ideas and ways. Each of the Greek writers had similar disregard for the cherished opinions of his Greek *confrères*. Singularly enough this independence is one of the most valuable features in all their procedure; for it reveals one of the great historical facts concerning all men in Jesus's day. That is to say that it reveals the great historical fact concerning Himself and His work that His people and He handled sacred Scriptures with perfect freedom; they altered them, and gave to the public, whom they taught devoutly, versions of those Scriptures quite different from the originals, and various versions of them quite different from each other. They all did so as a matter of duty, believing firmly that they themselves were inspired to do thus. When we read, as we often do, that Bible writers closed their writings by denouncing solemnly anyone who should ever alter the documents they had just written, we know that these denunciations simply point to the ingrained habit of the times. Every writing was sure to be altered.

(iii.) Esdras I. is a specially good illustration of this phenomenon of those early Jewish and Christian times. Even the old Hebrew-Aramaic book of Ezra was composed by piecing together, and somewhat rudely, portions of literature written by earlier hands, and even in different languages. And the reader soon finds that those sources, *e.g.*, the Hebrew Pentateuch and Samuel and Kings, had been very much altered by the compiler, and even made to say at times the opposite of the original stories.

By-and-by the Greek version-makers took like freedom. Probably our Esdras I. was one of the earliest of such versions, as we shall see presently. But its writer freely alters the original, and weaves in at least one long passage quite alien to the older book. Yet the version was counted so worthy, so good, and probably also so old, that it was used by the genuine and conservative Jew Josephus as his authority and source of information. Josephus repeats with full detail and full confidence that very portion which is so alien to the original 'Ezra.' It is a mere fancy to suppose that the people to whom our Lord belonged by nationality and by training were so conservative as to avoid or condemn all writings save the Hebrew canon.

Another version of 'Ezra' was made in Greek conforming more nearly to the Hebrew, and this is given in our present-day Greek Bible as Esdras; but it was long known as Esdras II. Our little pamphlet was held in most honour; and it was only about 200 A.D., when Christianity was becoming formal and ready to exalt something as a Divine law-book and rule of privilege, that then the 'Fathers' exercised severe hierarchical judgment, and cast our little Esdras out. They pronounced it 'apocryphal'; and then it came to be called 'Third Esdras,' for the titles 'First Esdras' and 'Second' were reserved for other Greek versions of 'Ezra' and 'Nehemiah,' which gained the preference and were allowed to stand in the ecclesiastically authoritative Septuagint Bible. But all this cannot alter the fact that the leading Jew Josephus had preferred this pamphlet of ours as a precious picture of his people and of God's care of them in both the past and his own present.

(iv.) We proceed now to sketch the pamphlet's contents.

(1.) In chap. i. 1-22 a great celebration of the Passover is described, and said to have been held under King Josiah. In detail—

(*a*) We are told that only then, *i.e.*, in 620 B.C., and by this king, was the 'Holy Ark' placed in the Temple built by Solomon.

(*b*) The Passover sacrifice is described as partly an oblation on an altar for burnt-offering, and partly a popular feast of flesh. Some of this food was roasted, but some was boiled into a tasty dish. The supply of food was prodigious, consuming 41,600 animals.

(*c*) A musical programme for the occasion was in the charge of the same singers and officials who are named as leaders in the Book of Psalms.

(*d*) From Samuel's day, it is said, *i.e.*, from before 1000 B.C. down to this date 620 B.C., no such Passover feast had ever been observed.

(2.) Chap. i. 23-33 tells the story of King Josiah's goodness, and his sad end.

(*a*) Pharaoh is described, without demur, as claiming that Iahweh, God of the Hebrews, was on the Egyptian's side, guiding him and helping him.

(*b*) The death of Josiah is located in Jerusalem, although 2 Kings says he died upon the battlefield of Megiddo in the north.

(3.) Chap. i. 34-58 records the misfortunes of the succeeding kings, the enslavement of the people and the ruin of the sanctuary, which lay desolate, we read, 'seventy years,' and 'until the Persians reigned.'

(*a*) This number of years is, of course, a traditional fancy, not equivalent even to the years from 599 B.C., the first captivity, ten years before the Temple fell, to 536 B.C., the fall of Babylon.

(*b*) The reference to the Persians marks the writer's date as very far away from the time when the Persians had held rule.

(4.) In chap. ii. 1-15 we read that Cyrus—who was king of Persia from 560 B.C., and of Babylon from 536 to 520 B.C.—proclaimed in his 'first year' that Iahweh had bidden him build His Temple in Jerusalem.

(*a*) Here begins the use of a peculiar, and late, name for Iahweh, viz., 'The Most High Lord.'

(*b*) The chief Judahites, Benjamites, priests and Levites in Babylon are said to have accepted universally the liberty to go to Zion and build.

(*c*) They were entrusted, we read, with all the deported sacred vessels, and carried all these back.

(*d*) The incorrect 'seventy years' of exile is again mentioned as the actual period of that slavery.

(5.) In chap. ii. 16-30 we come upon a strange disorder in story and doings and times. We find the writer passing at a bound from the reign of Cyrus (536-520 B.C.) across long years to the reign of an 'Artaxerxes.' This might be any one of three who bore that name: the first, reigning 465-425 B.C.—*i.e.*, sixty years later than Cyrus; the second, 404-358; and the third, 358-337. This displaced story, or 'erratic block' as geologists would say, tells how in Artaxerxes's time some Samaritan and other officers of that king caused the building of the Temple to stop. For they wrote to Artaxerxes condemning the work as a recrudescence of a rebellious folk. We notice in this tale that—

(*a*) The letter to the king, as reported, calls the former kings of Judah 'mighty and fierce potentates.' The aim of the story is more kindly than cruel; it means to magnify those 'potentates' and their people.

(*b*) Evidently, too, the writer wishes to condemn the Samaritans.

(*c*) But with all these aims he is naïvely unconcerned for consistency in his tale. For he says that the building was stopped from the time of Artaxerxes 'until the time of the King Darius.' But which Darius? Possibly the writer knew there was a Darius, the second king of the name, who ruled from 424 to 404 B.C.; and this Darius II. followed Artaxerxes I. And, furthermore, this second Darius lived about the traditionally supposed time of Ezra. But the compiler of the book meant Darius I., who lived before there was any Artaxerxes! The next following story shows that it was this Darius I., 520-485 B.C., who was in his mind.

(6.) For chaps. iii. 1 to v. 3 or 65 is an account of the doings of Zorobabel, who became governor of Judah under Darius I., and who was commissioned by that king to lead Jews—what Jews?—back to Judæa. Darius discovers Zorobabel through a famous trial of the poetic and philosophic exercises of the time. Really it was about Jesus's time that such were practised. Zorobabel and two others, young officers in the Persian army, contend in these, partly to soothe their royal master's insomnia. Zorobabel wins: for his reward he pleads for his people's freedom to go back to their old land and rebuild their city and sanctuary. Darius decrees that this be done. Now we find that—

(*a*) Darius sends to Jerusalem 'the deported sacred vessels,' although we had read that Cyrus had sent all these back already. Here, then, is what students call 'a doublet' in the document, and it is a good illustration of the methods of authors of those days. The writer found at least two parallel stories of the same return; he took no pains to reconstruct the 'history' that would underlie them both. His aim was quite another—namely, to glorify his nation, by telling how the great kings of old esteemed the race of Judah. So he simply pieced the two tales one after the other.

(*b*) The student of governmental methods and State economics will find here matters interesting to him.

(*c*) Musical instruments were much in use, at least in the writer's time; and they again correspond to those we read of in the Books of Psalms.

(*d*) Lists are given (v. 7-43) of persons said to have 'returned.' Such seem to have interested the writer much. And it is of great value for study of the development of Judaism to note how many classes of people and grades of hierarchical service had come into account. There is a great advance beyond the gradations mentioned in the Aaronic rules of Exodus. There are now priests, Levites, holy singers or Asaphites, porters, Temple servants, and Solomonites.

(*e*) Chap. v. 46 f. is repeated again in chap. ix. 37 f.

(*f*) A second 'doublet' (v. 4-6) is interesting. It is a fragment of a list, prefixed to the longer lists, and this fragment seems to have been inserted for the purpose of making prominent one 'Jesus,' *i.e.*, 'Joshua,' along with the Governor Zorobabel, or it may be his son. The point is of much value in the study of the reasons for the choice of our Saviour's name.

(*g*) The number of persons in the returning 'caravan' is astounding. Evidently the methods of the writer did not include critical sifting of such figures, and the times described were too far away to let exactness seem very important. The great aim, however, was to glorify the loved nation, and that in almost any way.

(*h*) Similarly uncritical and anachronous is the picture of a host of persons who are really in slavery in Babylon, and who bear nevertheless the names and designations of functionaries in the Temple of Jerusalem.

(*i*) The dates of the caravan's progress are noteworthy. It set out in spring, at the Babylonian New Year, which became the Jewish religious New Year time. By the autumn, when the old Palestinian New Year time came round, which has continned to this day to be the Jewish civil New Year's date, the people, as we read, had so far settled in Judah that they celebrated the great Vintage and Dance Feast. Then in the following year, in its second month, they laid their Temple's foundation stone with thanksgivings and with tears of joy. It is certainly a vivid tale, but the historicity limps. For example, they could scarcely have cultivated vineyards enough to have a real vintage feast within six months of their leaving Babylon. These little features mark the writer's thorough subjectivity; he is describing the ways of his own times, and not the past.

(*j*) Some people already dwelling in the land worshipped with them, but were oppressive.

(7.) *Another Doublet:* chap. v. 66-73.—Another story of delay, which lasted two years, and was caused by a conspiracy of people already in the land. The explanation of the collocation of these two stories is fairly clear.

(*a*) Strangely enough this delay is dated as far back as the days of Cyrus, and is said to have lasted until the days of Darius. One would suppose that the story of Zorobabel's pleasing the sleepless king, and the commission and return just described above, ought to have followed this story of delay.

(*b*) And yet, when the enemies wished to help to build the Temple, it was Zorobabel and Jesus who declined the aid, and so caused resentment and the delay.

(*c*) Evidently the compiler is simply piecing together his various materials, without regarding whether they be purely parallel stories of one event, and without care for an appearance at least of sequence. The great aim is to tell of repeated hindrances, and how they had all been surmounted by Providence and through the help of many princes, because this was the favoured people of God.

(8.) In chaps. vi. 1 to vii. 9 we read how in the days of Darius I. a fresh start in building operations was inspired by the prophets Haggai and Zechariah.

(*a*) But if we look into the books attributed to these two prophets we find that they are there credited indeed with inspiring the movement, but it is by rousing the well-to-do people, who might easily have been building long ago, and whose neglect had been punished by drought sent of God upon them. Our compiler has no mind to record any such faults.

(*b*) He rather does the opposite: for he tells another of his parallel stories of hindrance. This is caused by a Persian governor of Syria and Phœnicia, who is surprised over the building operations, and writes to his king, Darius, for orders.

(*c*) Our compiler has harked back now to the theory set forth in chap. ii (*see* p. xxv.), that it was King Cyrus who ordained the return, and that he sent back with it all the sacred vessels.

(*d*) To Darius the idea of return is new ; but he consults the archives of Cyrus, finds the old decree, and now renews in his own name the order to build the House of Iahweh.

(*e*) The Syrian governor receives the order, and now helps in the task.

(*f*) The completed Temple is dedicated with full services.

(*g*) We see thus again the compiler's steady purpose and method for exalting his nation.

(9.) Another Passover celebration is reported in chap. vii. 10-15.

(*a*) Comparison of its details with those of the Aaronic rules given in Exodus shows how progressive development took place.

(*b*) The joy of everybody over this festival is attributed to Iahweh's inclining the heart of 'the King of Assyria' to allow all these things. Evidently the 'Babylonian' captivity is so far away in the distant past, that the very name of the country of the old slavery is forgotten. Moreover, this Jewish compiler, an honoured man in our Lord's time, was evidently not compelled by the literary habit of his day to be at all carefully historical.

(*c*) But the Passover is exalted : that ceremony was clearly of much importance in the writer's time.

(10.) In chap. viii. 1 and on to ix. 36 we have the story of EZRA the priest, scribe, and expounder of the Torah or Doctrine of Iahweh. But this whole section seems interpolated.

(*a*) His genealogical line from the time of Aaron, say 1300 B.C. to that of Artaxerxes 450 B.C., is made to contain only sixteen generations. This cannot be correct.

(*b*) Ezra is described as leader of a pilgrimage from Babylon to Jerusalem with a missionary purpose. He went to teach his views of the Doctrine of Iahweh.

(*c*) This leader goes under a commission from King Artaxerxes, who permits to go with him any Jews, priests and Levites who wish to do so. Evidently the idea is that Zorobabel had by no means taken them all a hundred years before.

(*d*) But Ezra discovers that no priests and no Levites volunteer to emigrate with him. He invokes Divine help to win these, and some two hundred and fifty-eight are persuaded to go.

(*e*) The favour and help of Jehovah are represented as hard to obtain.

(*f*) Artaxerxes is credited with ordaining that in all respects, in the migration, and in Judah, the will of Iahweh, the Most High God, be obeyed.

(*g*) There is an eventful march and arrival.

(*h*) Ezra learns sorrowfully that Jews have been marrying Gentiles. A doctrine of an exclusive physically holy seed is taught.

(*i*) In a pathetic prayer Ezra appears as a very fountain and model of all morbid souls and all severe theologies. This illustrates exactly the society amid which our Lord proclaimed His Gospel.

(*j*) Ezra preaches a doctrine of divorce: and it is exactly what Jesus combated. And yet it marks a concentration of thought in those times upon the sacredness of marriage.

(II.) Chap. ix. 37-55 resumes the story of chap. v. 46 ff., and adds a good picture of synagogal exposition of Torah or doctrine.

(*a*) The passage is peculiarly interesting to the student of text, because the compiler has torn off the end of it. The last words, in the Greek, are the middle words of a sentence. The English translators have blurred this fact unwisely: and the verse should stand thus, 'And they assembled. . . .'

(*b*) The conclusion can be seen in the parallel copy of the story given in Neh. viii. 12, 13.

(*c*) The writer of this portion may be a Pharisee, for he makes Ezra, the Aaronitic scribe, teach even the priests.

(*d*) The picture of the assembly, the reading given probably in Hebrew, and the 'sense' or 'targum' given doubtless in Aramaic, are valuable.

(*e*) The occasion was festal and holy. It seems to have been the Vintage Dance Feast held in autumn.

The Faiths of the Authors and Readers of Esdras I.

(1.) They loved the Passover as virtually the greatest national religious service and the universal means of Jewish communion with God.

(2.) But they rejoiced also in the Vintage Dance Festival held six months later. These two feasts could be held everywhere. They were, moreover, both of them New Year celebrations, as we have seen.

(3.) The writers exercise perfect liberty to alter sacred Scriptures:—inspiration and authority to do so come to them, as to the saints of older time, although the great names of the past are very dear.

(4.) The times and people are devoted to literary activities.

(5.) They count the Jews worthy to receive honour and privileges from all kings and peoples, and they believe that their God will secure this.

(6.) But they believe the Jews must be a physically holy seed, although this should cost hurt to homes and human joys.

(7.) No great veneration is paid to priests and hierarchy. One writer at least may have been a Pharisee, or the age was losing care for sacerdotalism.

(8.) The conception of a 'Return from the Exile' is hazy, and the descriptions rather convey the idea that the rise of Judaism about 500 B.C. was due to the remnant who were left in the land, and not to emigrants from Babylon, save in so far as these from time to time emigrated to Judah to help those who were already there.

(9.) In conclusion, the heart of the writer is evidently often weary and hungry for the favour of God. The people listen eagerly to the preacher, and wonder how to please Him who is in Heaven. The writers of Esdras I. are just the men, and those about them are the men, to whom Jesus said, 'Come unto Me. I will give you rest.'

ANALYSIS OF ESDRAS II.

(i.) Here we are in quite another atmosphere. Passing from the audience of the Scribe of First Esdras to the Visions of the Seer of Esdras Second, we are certainly in the same Jewish land; but the sky has become overcast and darker far, yet with great gleams and flashes around and overhead. We have left the times of fairly comfortable exposition of past glories, and the weariness within that might be somewhat hidden. Storm is beating about us now.

Yet just in the storm the flash reveals the treasure. Here sit souls, battling with fightings within, and amid terrible fears, ay, and ruins without; but, by common consent of all who study the pages of this apocalypse, the dreamer who utters it is one of the noblest of Jews or of men, of thinkers and of fear-less God-fearing souls. Strange it may seem, but true it is, that Jewish character, like its ancestral Hebrew spirit, has always shone out most brightly and beautifully when under oppression. From the very flint of their nature the iron blow on this people has always struck out light and fire. Amos sprang to speech amid the beginnings of distress: Jeremiah rose to his boldness and nobility out of more woeful depths: the Slave who sang Isa. liii. chanted of Life and Forgiveness over the grave of the Man of Sorrows. When those Hebrews had all fallen, then Judaism began, low down and childish; but it rose with great bursts of inspiration, until, under the crushing heel of Antiochus, the fragrance of the 'Daniel' book was poured out in the faith and the cry that

> 'God enters into and shares the sufferings of His saints.'

Then soon again the hard-pressed dissenter from the Hasmonæan rule, with its non-Davidic state and its non-Mosaic church, bowed his head and sang:—

> 'My God, my God, why hast Thou forsaken me!'
>
> . . . .
>
> 'O Thou, my Succour, haste Thou to help me!'

In Jesus's times and throughout His century the two forms of literature, Apocalypse and Psalmody, were abundant, and ex-pressed the mind and heart of two extremes in society. While Psalmody was the utterance of the finer men of culture, away at the other end the Apocalyptic Vision was the wonted way of discourse among the genuinely honest but far more childlike enthusiasts. The New Testament writers talk of many of these almost wild visionaries. While the Psalmists communed with the speechful silences of God, the Apocalyptists or Revelation-writers dreamed, imagined, conceived marvels of material blisses that Iahweh would give to His people. They rose at times to such boundless phantasy that immediately the seers themselves felt they must give interpretations of their visions, if they were to be of any use at all. So did they try to solve the riddles and the hard fates of the soul and of the world.

There were many who wrote such apocalypses. They have given us the books of Daniel, of Enoch, and of John, and more. But among them none rises to such height and power as does the seer of Esdras II.; no other pierces so far to find, if possible, the centre of life's labyrinth. His faith is to be likened to nothing less intense than that of Paul, if we conceive of that Apostle as wrestling with the God of his fathers, and determined, according to his own description in Rom. vii., to compel heaven as well as earth to give him peace. Esdras II. is just a Paul before he could write that Epistle, and before he laid his hand on the master-key of all things, by grasping the hand of the Crucified One, as he sobbed out:—

'My Lord and my God, I know Thee now!'

We may well quote from perhaps the finest writer of late years on the little book, Professor H. Gunkel (*see* Kautzsch's *Apocrypha and Pseudepigrapha of the O.T.*, Vol. II. p. 402 ff.): 'These are experiences (in Esdras II.) that Paul must have passed through before his conversion. . . . The author is far removed from the deliverance Paul found. . . . Yet his agonizing before God's face for the weal of his soul is truly honourable and pathetic.' Here, then, in Esdras II., we have an autograph of a Jew who did not grasp Christian faith like the Apostle, but who rose to the highest spiritual attainment that was otherwise possible. He could only feed his soul's hunger with apocalyptic hope; but he was indeed 'not far from seeing the Divine Kingdom.'

(ii.) The man uttered this faith in the days of the early Christians, and in the hearing of them, say between 90 and 100 B.C.

(*a*) For we shall see presently, in the Fifth of the Seven Visions of the book, that its writer lived under the Emperor Domitian, and his predecessor Titus had just been destroyed. He himself says he wrote 'thirty years after the city fell.'

(*b*) It was written for Jews, and was at first in the Hebrew tongue. It attacks Christianity on some crucial points. Yet it has comparatively small interest in that new religion, and is most profoundly concerned for the Jewish future both in this world and the next. The writer believed firmly in these two Ages or Æons, Here and Hereafter. He was a Pharisee, and a thorough opponent of Sadduceeism.

(*c*) But it was adopted by Christians, and its faiths figured soon among the Christian schemes of theology, as some of them do to this day. By-and-by, say within two hundred years, the book was made more Christian in look by fitting it with a preface—the present chaps. i. and ii.—written probably, says Mr James in his Introduction to Bensly's Text, by a hand that wrote another Christian apocalypse, attributed to Zephaniah. And a less decidedly Christian Appendix was prepared specially for the book about 268 A.D., says Mr. James. Such adaptations and additions were very common in those days.

(*d*) Strangely enough, the Hebrew original has been lost. Gunkel's suggested explanation is opportune. He attributes the misfortune to the despair of the Jews when the Jewish State was finally ruined in the days of the Emperor Hadrian, 135 A.D.

That visitation of Providence might induce the Jews, through fear, to withdraw affection and reverence from all writings not in the old Hebrew Collection or directly connected with it. We know that the book of Enoch also was similarly lost. Indeed, apocalypse was suspected always by the authoritative Jews, for 'Daniel' hardly got admission into the Sacred Collection.

(*e*) But the Greek translation was lost also, and there is none existing save one made lately by Hilgenfeld, de Lagarde, and Röusch. Gunkel suggests again a cause in the fear of philosophic Greek Christian Fathers lest apocalyptic literature might teach the churches to like Oriental mythologies. So the churches in the more central and Greek provinces threw away the little book, and it was only in the far off barbarian churches in lands like Italy, Syria, Armenia and Ethiopia that translations were preserved. And we have their versions to this day. In far-excluded Arabia even two quite different versions were loved and handed on to us.

(*f*) But a strange fate befel the Latin translation! All save four of the many MSS. of it lack chap. vii. 35-105; and no one of these four was generally known before the year 1865. Up till then the seventy verses had to be supplied from the Oriental versions; but in that year it was discovered that a whole leaf had been cut out long ago from the MS. that belonged to St. Germains, near Paris, and this leaf corresponded exactly to those lost seventy verses. Evidently it was from that mutilated MS. that all the others had been copied, save, indeed, the four which now began to come out of their hiding-places. Oddly enough, the copies of the faulty book had been made chiefly by Englishmen some 700 years ago, and now the discovery of the four good copies was due chiefly to our countryman, the late Professor Bensly. His story of his work reads like a romance.

But why had the leaf been cut away and lost? Not for the oft-given reason that it condemned Prayers for the Dead, else much more would have been excised, since such condemnation goes on in the following portions of the MS. It may be said, with all reverence, that the lost and found pages read almost like a first draft of Dante's *Divine Comedy*. One cannot help wondering whether that leaf with its First Century Vision was ever carried to Florence.

(iii.) This book of Visions is imputed to Ezra: and good men learned to call it 'apocryphal,' or, what seems even worse, 'a Pseudepigraph,' a 'falsely-imputed' book! But the reader soon sees that its author was a man without guile, unable to be false. He believed he was writing just what Ezra would have said, and what that ancestral saint must have seen in the visions of his soul. It was exactly the like faith that made another writer impute to Moses the opinion, recorded in Exod. vi., that Iahweh, the God of Israel, was never known before the Exodus! The method was orthodox in its day; and more, it was perfectly and spiritually natural. It was born of faith that the God who was felt to be present with the author of such writings had been the God of the Fathers, and the same God inspired His people from everlasting to everlasting.

As for the number, 'Second' or otherwise, added to the title, it is sufficient to quote M. R. James's Introduction to Bensly's Text of our booklet, p. xxv. f. He says chaps. iii. to xiv. are called:—

The First Book of Ezra, in the better Arabic Version and in the Ethiopic Version;

The Second Book of Ezra, in some Latin MSS. and in the English A.V., which follows the Genevan Bible in this particular;

The Third Book of Ezra, in the Armenian Version (apparently), and by Ambrose of Milan in his *De Spiritu Sancto*;

The Fourth Book of Ezra, by most of the Latin MSS., including that of St. Germains and that of Amiens.

(iv.) We may outline the work briefly now, *i.e.*, the real book, chaps. iii. to xiv. only. It consists of Seven Visions. They were received by one Salathiel, who is also called Ezra, and he had sought them and prepared himself in special ways to receive them. His way of obtaining inspiration throws light on the whole conception of inspiration in those times. The visions came 'in the thirtieth year after the destruction of the city,' that is presumably Jerusalem; which agrees fairly with the date obtained from Vision Fifth.

(I.) The First Vision occupies chaps. iii. to v. 19. In it—

(1.) Esdras asks God why He has made all the world's sin and sorrow? All men, from Adam on, Jews and Romans, are created with a sinful disposition, save a few exceptions easily to be counted.

(2.) The Angel of Light answers that many problems are beyond man's solving.

(3.) Esdras cries in agony, 'Why, then, was understanding given to me?' and 'What will God do for my people who are all called by His name?'

(4.) The Angel answers that this World, or Age, or Æon, is fast passing away, and the next age will bring the solutions.

(5.) That age shall dawn at once when the number of the Elect Righteous is fulfilled. We may see here the source of some phrases in the Anglican Prayer-Book.

(6.) The signs of the End are recounted much as Matt. xxiv. gives them.

(7.) Evidently the writer is picturing the wrestlings and hopes born within his own thinking.

(II.) The Second Vision (v. 20-vi. 34) follows after seven days of further preparation.

(1.) Esdras pleads that God chose His people, and endowed them with all choicest gifts, especially with His own Torah or doctrine. Why should these, just these, be trodden under foot of all men?

(2.) The Angel answers that God loves His people at least as much as Esdras does.

(3.) In a fine passage the Angel asks, 'Canst thou show me the image of a Voice? No more canst thou solve all that God understands.'

(4.) It is specially declared that the Final Judgment and Solution of all these problems shall be the act of God Himself alone. No other shall share this. Here seems a polemic against the early Christian doctrine, that the Son of Man and the saints shall judge the world.

(5.) More tokens of the end are described much as in John's Revelation.

(III.) The Third Vision (vi. 35-ix. 25) is obtained after another seven days of fasting. It is perhaps the finest in conception, and full of loftiest thought, among all the Seven.

(1.) It sets forth the wonders of Creation, and the faith that all this was performed for the sake of God's people; and then the problem is set and searched, 'Why do not Iahweh's people possess the world?'

(2.) The Angel says that the people tread indeed a strait and difficult road now; but this leads to a better future.

(3.) But a second answer given is of utmost interest. It is that the Coming Age is to be brought in by God's Own Anointed Son, His Christ. He shall reign through four hundred years of bliss: then He shall die: He shall rise again: all the dead shall awake: then the Most High God will hold His Great Judgment. In some MSS. the name 'Jesus' is given to Him, but this may be interpolated.

(4.) Then follows the long lost passage (vii. 36-105). This tells how few shall obtain the second and final bliss.

(5.) To the question whether there shall be an intermediate state of conscious rest between the first death and the resurrection, an answer is given that reads like a sketch of Dante's *Purgatorio*.

(6.) In the latter part of the lost and found passage, and running on also into the following pages, is a discussion whether intercession for the departed is justified. The decision is, that it is not so. The person who wrought the mutilation was, however, evidently indifferent on this question.

(7.) In chap. vii. 48 [118] ff. is a pathetic cry to Adam, reproaching him for the sin and sorrow of all men. And the heart of the writer is tender to far more souls than to the Jews alone. He bewails the sore sad lot of all men.

(8.) An exquisite passage follows (vii. 62 [132] ff.): it is a glad meditation, based, one might think, on Exod. xxxiv. 5 ff., concerning the compassion, long-suffering, and forgiving goodness of God. This Character of God is the writer's assurance that He will help and save an innumerable multitude of souls. One might almost count the writer a companion of Jesus and of Paul in thought and faith.

(9.) A prayer following these passages (viii. 20-36) has often been copied by itself alone, and called 'Esdras's Confession.' It is, however, more severe than the previous passage. To a cry like the old word, 'Shall not the Judge of all the earth do right?' answers are given that rise finally to great tenderness and power.

(IV.) The Fourth Vision (ix. 26-x. 59) expounds a theory of 'The Holy Kingdom Israel.'

(1.) The theory is set forth in an allegory and its interpretation. A wife, being childless, who is Zion, bears at length a Son, the Kingdom: He waxes into years, weds, dies on his espousal night; this signifies the sad ruin of Jerusalem. Evidently the writer counted the time just before 70 A.D., the time of Judaism's highest happiness.

(2.) The style of the work is changing here. The agony amid perplexities is somewhat past. The method is more visionary. Some fine lyric passages occur.

(V.) The Fifth Vision (xi. 1-xii. 51) is also of the more visionary sort: it is again a dream with its interpretation.

(1.) Esdras sees a wonderful eagle, many-winged, three-headed, which rules the earth, uttering its voice: But another voice speaks: Then another voice approaches, it is a roaring lion: The eagle falls and is burned: The earth is full of fear.

(2.) By interpretation the three heads are three kings: The third slays the second, and these latter two are probably Titus and Domitian. Then The Christ comes, reproves, destroys all men, save His own people.

(3.) 'The rest of His people shall He deliver with mercy.

. . . He shall make them joyful until the coming of the end, even the Day of Judgment.' This shows how closely parallel were the conceptions and teachings of Judaism on the one hand and early Christianity on the other.

(VI.) The Sixth Vision (chap. xiii.) gives another dream and its interpretation, which set forth the nature and task of The Christ as the Jews desired Him.

(1.) A man rises from the sea, which means 'from the Unseen.'

(2.) His appearance and His ways are much like the corresponding features described in the Revelations of Daniel and of John.

(3.) His task is to face a host of enemies: to war against them, and yet without any other weapon than His Voice: He annihilates them all.

(4.) Some features of the doctrine mark it off distinctly from most Christian theories. Of course, the Christian Christ is generally regarded as a Saviour and not a Destroyer. Yet some large sections of Christendom have also taught that He is to be a Destroyer.

(*a*) But, further, Esdras II. teaches that those who remain on the earth until the Coming of this Anointed Son of God are more blessed than the dead. This view was often opposed by early Christians.

(*b*) The Jewish Christ is to reassemble the lost Ten Tribes: for all of these repented long ago, and have kept the Deuteronomic statutes during their long exile.

(*c*) 'No man on earth can see this Son of God or His companions until the time of His glorious coming.' This is surely intended as a polemic against Christianity.

(VII.) The Seventh and Final Vision (chap. xiv.) is a doctrine or 'legend' of the Restoration of the Sacred Scriptures, through an inspiration of Esdras for this service.

(1.) It repeats the faith that Moses received some oracles that he was to conceal, as well as some that he was to reveal.

(2.) But, it is held, all of them have been burned in the burned city. This is probably an outgrowth of the fact that all Hebrew MSS. of the Old Testament save one were destroyed about this date in some way; and this one MS. has furnished all the extant copies, which are virtually facsimile of each other. The doctrine is also a fruit of the tradition that Ezra brought the 'Teaching' from Babylon to Jerusalem about the year 440 B.C.

(3.) The present World, or Age, or Æon, is nearly ended; scarcely one-sixth of it is yet to be. Therefore the lost oracles are to be restored.

(4.) In forty days Esdras is to dictate to five scribes the ninety-four books of the oracles.

(5.) Esdras receives inspiration for this task partly by a Lamp of Wisdom set of God within his mind, and partly by a Draught from a fiery, full cup.

(6.) Twenty-four of the books are the well-known Hebrew Collection, Maccabees and the like Greek books being excluded. The remaining books, a perfect seventy, very much richer and larger than the twenty-four, contain the further oracles which Moses was to conceal, and which God means yet to give.

(7.) These seventy are to be entrusted by Esdras to 'the wise men,' for these have the well-spring of Understanding, the fountain of Wisdom and the stream of Knowledge. They will publish these oracles in due time.

(8.) Esdras performs all this in his own forty-first year, and in the twelfth day of the third month of the year 5000 from the creation of the world. The sentence recording this has been lost from the Latin MSS., but is given in the Oriental versions.

(9.) Then speedily Esdras is translated; and he is thenceforth accounted 'The Scribe of the Highest Wisdom for ever and ever.'

Of the Doctrines or Religious Views of Esdras II.

We may easily summarise these as follows:—

(1.) Original Sin was created in Adam, and has cursed all men pitifully and mysteriously.

(2.) Yet a studious soul may wrestle with God for light and guidance; and may receive these by methods within men's reach.

(3.) The Wise possess more Divine Revelations than have been given in the Sacred Collection; and they shall reveal these wisely to all men.

(4.) God will anoint a Man, who shall be His Son, and who shall accomplish God's purposes on earth, warring by His Words to the destruction of all the enemies of Israel.

(5.) All the dead shall rise again with this Christ to bliss or to woe: The final fates shall be awarded by the Most High God alone, no one sharing with Him His Work of Judgment.

(6.) A true elect soul is full of tenderness and compassion for all souls: and so is God.

(7.) But none may pray for the dead.

(8.) In the new World or Age soon to dawn there shall be Dantean circles on circles of blisses, of purgations, and of woes.

The Books of Esdras

Of the Prefixed and Appended Chapters.

(1.) Chaps. i. and ii. are a Christian lament much akin to Matt. xxiii. f.

(2.) Chaps. xv. and xvi. are a fearful prophecy concerning all unbelievers. They seem like an effort to supplement the woes pronounced by Esdras, but to turn the whole against non-Christians. The portion dates probably from two hundred years after the Jewish work was composed.

The First Book of Esdras

The Passover of Josias

AND Josias held the feast of the passover in Jerusalem unto his Lord, and offered the passover the fourteenth day of the first month; having set the priests according to their daily courses, being arrayed in long garments, in the temple of the Lord. And he spake unto the Levites, the holy ministers of Israel, that they should hallow themselves unto the Lord, to set the holy ark of the Lord in the house that king Solomon the son of David had built!

And said, Ye shall no more bear the ark upon your shoulders: now therefore serve the Lord your God, and minister unto his people Israel, and prepare you after your families and kindreds, according as David the king of Israel prescribed, and according to the magnificence of Solomon his son: and standing in the temple according to the several dignity of the families of you the Levites, who minister in the presence of your brethren the children of Israel, offer the passover in order, and make ready the sacrifices for your brethren, and keep the passover according to the commandment of the Lord, which was given unto Moses. And unto the people that

The Offering of Josias

was found there Josias gave thirty thousand lambs and kids, and three thousand calves: these things were given of the king's allowance, according as he promised, to the people, to the priests, and to the Levites. And Helkias, Zacharias, and Syelus, the governors of the temple, gave to the priests for the passover two thousand and six hundred sheep, and three hundred calves. And Jeconias, and Samaias, and Nathanael his brother, and Assabias, and Ochiel, and Joram, captains over thousands, gave to the Levites for the passover five thousand sheep, and seven hundred calves.

And when these things were done, the priests and Levites, having the unleavened bread, stood in very comely order according to the kindreds, and according to the several dignities of the fathers, before the people, to offer to the Lord, as it is written in the book of Moses: and thus did they in the morning. And they roasted the passover with fire, as appertaineth: as for the sacrifices, they sod them in brass pots and pans with a good savour, and set them before all the people: and afterward they prepared for themselves, and for the priests their brethren, the sons of Aaron. For the priests offered the fat until night: and the Levites prepared for themselves, and the priests their brethren, the sons of Aaron. The holy singers also, the sons of Asaph, were in their order, according to the appointment of David, to wit, Asaph, Zacharias, and Jeduthun, who was of the

Character of Josias

king's retinue. Moreover the porters were at every gate; it was not lawful for any to go from his ordinary service: for their brethren the Levites prepared for them.

Thus were the things that belonged to the sacrifices of the Lord accomplished in that day, that they might hold the passover, and offer sacrifices upon the altar of the Lord, according to the commandment of king Josias. So the children of Israel which were present held the passover at that time, and the feast of sweet bread seven days. And such a passover was not kept in Israel since the time of the prophet Samuel. Yea, all the kings of Israel held not such a passover as Josias, and the priests, and the Levites, and the Jews, held with all Israel that were found dwelling at Jerusalem. In the eighteenth year of the reign of Josias was this passover kept.

And the works of Josias were upright before his Lord with an heart full of godliness. As for the things that came to pass in his time, they were written in former times, concerning those that sinned, and did wickedly against the Lord above all people and kingdoms, and how they grieved him exceedingly, so that the words of the Lord rose up against Israel.

Now after all these acts of Josias it came to pass, that Pharaoh the king of Egypt came to raise war at Carchamis upon Euphrates: and Josias went out against him. But the king of Egypt sent to him,

Death of Josias

saying, What have I to do with thee, O king of Judea? I am not sent out from the Lord God against thee; for my war is upon Euphrates: and now the Lord is with me, yea, the Lord is with me hasting me forward: depart from me, and be not against the Lord. Howbeit Josias did not turn back his chariot from him, but undertook to fight with him, not regarding the words of the prophet Jeremy spoken by the mouth of the Lord: but joined battle with him in the plain of Magiddo, and the princes came against king Josias.

Then said the king unto his servants, Carry me away out of the battle; for I am very weak. And immediately his servants took him away out of the battle. Then gat he up upon his second chariot; and being brought back to Jerusalem died, and was buried in his father's sepulchre. And in all Jewry they mourned for Josias, yea, Jeremy the prophet lamented for Josias, and the chief men with the women made lamentation for him unto this day: and this was given out for an ordinance to be done continually in all the nation of Israel. These things are written in the book of the stories of the kings of Judah, and every one of the acts that Josias did, and his glory, and his understanding in the law of the Lord, and the things that he had done before, and the things now recited, are reported in the book of the kings of Israel and Judea.

And the people took Joachaz the son of Josias,

The Babylonian Captivity

and made him king instead of Josias his father, when he was twenty and three years old. And he reigned in Judea and in Jerusalem three months: and then the king of Egypt deposed him from reigning in Jerusalem. And he set a tax upon the land of an hundred talents of silver and one talent of gold. The king of Egypt also made king Joacim his brother king of Judea and Jerusalem. And he bound Joacim and the nobles: but Zaraces his brother he apprehended, and brought him out of Egypt.

Five and twenty years old was Joacim when he was made king in the land of Judea and Jerusalem; and he did evil before the Lord. Wherefore against him Nabuchodonosor the king of Babylon came up, and bound him with a chain of brass, and carried him into Babylon. Nabuchodonosor also took of the holy vessels of the Lord, and carried them away, and set them in his own temple at Babylon. But those things that are recorded of him, and of his uncleanness and impiety, are written in the chronicles of the kings. And Joacim his son reigned in his stead: he was made king being eighteen years old; and reigned but three months and ten days in Jerusalem; and did evil before the Lord.

So after a year Nabuchodonosor sent and caused him to be brought into Babylon with the holy vessels of the Lord; and made Zedechias king of Judea and Jerusalem, when he was one and twenty years old; and he reigned eleven years: and he did evil also in

Jerusalem during the Exile

the sight of the Lord, and cared not for the words that were spoken unto him by the prophet Jeremy from the mouth of the Lord. And after that king Nabuchodonosor had made him to swear by the name of the Lord, he forswore himself, and rebelled; and hardening his neck, and his heart, he transgressed the laws of the Lord God of Israel. The governors also of the people and of the priests did many things against the laws, and passed all the pollutions of all nations, and defiled the temple of the Lord, which was sanctified in Jerusalem.

Nevertheless the God of their fathers sent by his messenger to call them back, because he spared them and his tabernacle also. But they had his messengers in derision; and, look, when the Lord spake unto them, they made a sport of his prophets: so far forth, that he, being wroth with his people for their great ungodliness, commanded the kings of the Chaldees to come up against them; who slew their young men with the sword, yea, even within the compass of their holy temple, and spared neither young man nor maid, old man nor child, among them; for he delivered all into their hands. And they took all the holy vessels of the Lord, both great and small, with the vessels of the ark of God, and the king's treasures, and carried them away into Babylon.

As for the house of the Lord, they burnt it, and brake down the walls of Jerusalem, and set fire upon her towers: and as for her glorious things, they

The Actio of Cyrus

never ceased till they had consumed and brought them all to nought: and the people that were not slain with the sword he carried unto Babylon: who became servants to him and his children, till the Persians reigned, to fulfil the word of the Lord spoken by the mouth of Jeremy: until the land had enjoyed her sabbaths, the whole time of her desolation shall she rest, until the full term of seventy years. * In the first year of Cyrus king of the Persians, that the word of the Lord might be accomplished, that he had promised by the mouth of Jeremy; the Lord raised up the spirit of Cyrus the king of the Persians, and he made proclamation through all his kingdom, and also by writing, saying, Thus saith Cyrus king of the Persians; the Lord of Israel, the most high Lord, hath made me king of the whole world, and commanded me to build him an house at Jerusalem in Jewry. If therefore there be any of you that are of his people, let the Lord, even his Lord, be with him, and let him go up to Jerusalem that is in Judea, and build the house of the Lord of Israel: for he is the Lord that dwelleth in Jerusalem. Whosoever then dwell in the places about, let them help him, those, I say, that are his neighbours, with gold, and with silver, with gifts, with horses, and with cattle, and other things, which have been set forth by vow, for the temple of the Lord at Jerusalem.

Then the chief of the families of Judea and of the tribe of Benjamin stood up; the priests also, and the

Cyrus restores the Temple Vessels

Levites, and all they whose mind the Lord had moved to go up, and to build an house for the Lord at Jerusalem, and they that dwelt round about them, and helped them in all things with silver and gold, with horses and cattle, and with very many free gifts of a great number whose minds were stirred up thereto. King Cyrus also brought forth the holy vessels, which Nabuchodonosor had carried away from Jerusalem, and had set up in his temple of idols.

Now when Cyrus king of the Persians had brought them forth, he delivered them to Mithridates his treasurer: and by him they were delivered to Sanabassar the governor of Judea. And this was the number of them; A thousand golden cups, and a thousand of silver, censers of silver twenty nine, vials of gold thirty, and of silver two thousand four hundred and ten, and a thousand other vessels. So all the vessels of gold and of silver, which were carried away, were five thousand four hundred threescore and nine. These were brought back by Sanabassar, together with them of the captivity, from Babylon to Jerusalem.

But in the time of Artaxerxes king of the Persians Belemus, and Mithridates, and Tabellius, and Rathumus, and Beeltethmus, and Semellius the secretary, with others that were in commission with them, dwelling in Samaria and other places, wrote unto him against them that dwelt in Judea and Jerusalem these letters following; To king Artaxerxes our lord, Thy servants, Rathumus the storywriter, and

The Samaritans are Angry

Semellius the scribe, and the rest of their council, and the judges that are in Celosyria and Phenice. Be it now known to the lord the king, that the Jews that are come up from you to us, being come into Jerusalem, that rebellious and wicked city, do build the marketplaces, and repair the walls of it, and do lay the foundation of the temple. Now if this city and the walls thereof be made up again, they will not only refuse to give tribute, but also rebel against kings. And forasmuch as the things pertaining to the temple are now in hand, we think it meet not to neglect such a matter, but to speak unto our lord the king, to the intent that, if it be thy pleasure, it may be sought out in the books of thy fathers: and thou shalt find in the chronicles what is written concerning these things, and shalt understand that that city was rebellious, troubling both kings and cities: and that the Jews were rebellious, and raised always wars therein; for the which cause even this city was made desolate. Wherefore now we do declare unto thee, O lord the king, that if this city be built again, and the walls thereof set up anew, thou shalt from henceforth have no passage into Celosyria and Phenice.

Then the king wrote back again to Rathumus the storywriter, to Beeltethmus, to Semellius the scribe, and to the rest that were in commission, and dwellers in Samaria and Syria and Phenice, after this manner; I have read the epistle which ye have sent unto me: therefore I commanded to make diligent search, and

They write to Artaxerxes to stop the Work

it hath been found that that city was from the beginning practising against kings; and the men therein were given to rebellion and war: and that mighty kings and fierce were in Jerusalem, who reigned and exacted tributes in Celosyria and Phenice. Now therefore I have commanded to hinder those men from building the city, and heed to be taken that there be no more done in it; and that those wicked workers proceed no further to the annoyance of kings. Then king Artaxerxes his letters being read, Rathumus, and Semellius the scribe, and the rest that were in commission with them, removing in haste towards Jerusalem with a troop of horsemen and a multitude of people in battle array, began to hinder the builders; and the building of the temple in Jerusalem ceased until the second year of the reign of Darius king of the Persians.

* Now when Darius reigned, he made a great feast unto all his subjects, and unto all his household, and unto all the princes of Media and Persia, and to all the governors and captains and lieutenants that were under him, from India unto Ethiopia, of an hundred twenty and seven provinces. And when they had eaten and drunken, and being satisfied were gone home, then Darius the king went into his bedchamber, and slept, and soon after awaked.

Then three young men, that were of the guard that kept the king's body, spake one to another; Let every one of us speak a sentence: he that shall

The Three Writings

overcome, and whose sentence shall seem wiser than the others, unto him shall the king Darius give great gifts, and great things in token of victory: as, to be clothed in purple, to drink in gold, and to sleep upon gold, and a chariot with bridles of gold, and an head-tire of fine linen, and a chain about his neck: and he shall sit next to Darius because of his wisdom, and shall be called Darius his cousin. And then every one wrote his sentence, sealed it, and laid it under king Darius his pillow; and said that, when the king is risen, some will give him the writings; and of whose side the king and the three princes of Persia shall judge that his sentence is the wisest, to him shall the victory be given, as was appointed.

The first wrote, Wine is the strongest.

The second wrote, The king is strongest.

The third wrote, Women are strongest: but above all things Truth beareth away the victory.

Now when the king was risen up, they took their writings, and delivered them unto him, and so he read them: and sending forth he called all the princes of Persia and Media, and the governors, and the captains, and the lieutenants, and the chief officers; and sat him down in the royal seat of judgment; and the writings were read before them. And he said, Call the young men, and they shall declare their own sentences. So they were called, and came in. And he said unto them, Declare unto us your mind concerning the writings.

Speeches of the Young Men

Then began the first, who had spoken of the strength of wine; and he said thus, O ye men, how exceeding strong is wine! it causeth all men to err that drink it: it maketh the mind of the king and of the fatherless child to be all one; of the bondman and of the freeman, of the poor man and of the rich: it turneth also every thought into jollity and mirth, so that a man remembereth neither sorrow nor debt: and it maketh every heart rich, so that a man remembereth neither king nor governor; and it maketh to speak all things by talents: and when they are in their cups, they forget their love both to friends and brethren, and a little after draw out swords: but when they are from the wine, they remember not what they have done. O ye men, is not wine the strongest, that enforceth to do thus? And when he had so spoken, he held his peace.

* Then the second, that had spoken of the strength of the king, began to say, O ye men, do not men excel in strength, that bear rule over sea and land, and all things in them? But yet the king is more mighty: for he is lord of all these things, and hath dominion over them; and whatsoever he commandeth them they do. If he bid them make war the one against the other, they do it: if he send them out against the enemies, they go, and break down mountains, walls, and towers. They slay and are slain, and transgress not the king's commandment: if they get the victory, they bring all to the king, as

Speeches of the Young Men

well the spoil, as all things else. Likewise for those that are no soldiers, and have not to do with wars, but use husbandry, when they have reaped again that which they had sown, they bring it to the king, and compel one another to pay tribute unto the king. And yet he is but one man: if he command to kill, they kill; if he command to spare, they spare; if he command to smite, they smite; if he command to make desolate, they make desolate; if he command to build, they build; if he command to cut down, they cut down; if he command to plant, they plant. So all his people and his armies obey him: furthermore he lieth down, he eateth and drinketh, and taketh his rest: and these keep watch round about him, neither may any one depart, and do his own business, neither disobey they him in any thing. O ye men, how should not the king be mightiest, when in such sort he is obeyed? And he held his tongue.

Then the third, who had spoken of women, and of the truth, (this was Zorobabel) began to speak. O ye men, it is not the great king, nor the multitude of men, neither is it wine, that excelleth; who is it then that ruleth them, or hath the lordship over them? are they not women? Women have borne the king and all the people that bear rule by sea and land. Even of them came they: and they nourished them up that planted the vineyards, from whence the wine cometh. These also make garments for men; these bring glory unto men; and without women cannot

The Third Speaker: the Power of Women

men be. Yea, and if men have gathered together gold and silver, or any other goodly thing, do they not love a woman which is comely in favour and beauty? And letting all those things go, do they not gape, and even with open mouth fix their eyes fast on her; and have not all men more desire unto her than unto silver or gold, or any goodly thing whatsoever? A man leaveth his own father that brought him up, and his own country, and cleaveth unto his wife. He sticketh not to spend his life with his wife, and remembereth neither father, nor mother, nor country. By this also ye must know that women have dominion over you: do ye not labour and toil, and give and bring all to the woman? Yea, a man taketh his sword, and goeth his way to rob and to steal, to sail upon the sea and upon rivers; and looketh upon a lion, and goeth in the darkness; and when he hath stolen, spoiled, and robbed, he bringeth it to his love. Wherefore a man loveth his wife better than father or mother. Yea, many there be that have run out of their wits for women, and become servants for their sakes. Many also have perished, have erred, and sinned, for women. And now do ye not believe me? is not the king great in his power? do not all regions fear to touch him? Yet did I see him and Apame the king's concubine, the daughter of the admirable Bartacus, sitting at the right hand of the king, and taking the crown from the king's head, and setting it upon her own

The Glor of Truth

head; she also struck the king with her left hand. And yet for all this the king gaped and gazed upon her with open mouth: if she laughed upon him, he laughed also: but if she took any displeasure at him, the king was fain to flatter, that she might be reconciled to him again. O ye men, how can it be but women should be strong, seeing they do thus?

Then the king and the princes looked one upon another: so he began to speak of the truth. O ye men, are not women strong? great is the earth, high is the heaven, swift is the sun in his course, for he compasseth the heavens round about, and fetcheth his course again to his own place in one day. Is he not great that maketh these things? therefore great is the truth, and stronger than all things. All the earth calleth upon the truth, and the heaven blesseth it: all works shake and tremble at it, and with it is no unrighteous thing. Wine is wicked, the king is wicked, women are wicked, all the children of men are wicked, and such are all their wicked works; and there is no truth in them; in their unrighteousness also they shall perish. As for the truth, it endureth, and is always strong; it liveth and conquereth for evermore. With her there is no accepting of persons or rewards; but she doeth the things that are just, and refraineth from all unjust and wicked things; and all men do well like of her works. Neither in her judgment is any unrighteousness; and she is the strength, kingdom, power, and

The King reminded of his Vow

majesty, of all ages. Blessed be the God of truth. And with that he held his peace. And all the people then shouted, and said, Great is Truth, and mighty above all things.

Then said the king unto him, Ask what thou wilt more than is appointed in the writing, and we will give it thee, because thou art found wisest; and thou shalt sit next me, and shalt be called my cousin.

Then said he unto the king, Remember thy vow, which thou hast vowed to build Jerusalem, in the day when thou camest to thy kingdom, and to send away all the vessels that were taken away out of Jerusalem, which Cyrus set apart, when he vowed to destroy Babylon, and to send them again thither. Thou also hast vowed to build up the temple, which the Edomites burned when Judea was made desolate by the Chaldees. And now, O lord the king, this is that which I require, and which I desire of thee, and this is the princely liberality proceeding from thyself: I desire therefore that thou make good the vow, the performance whereof with thine own mouth thou hast vowed to the King of heaven.

Then Darius the king stood up, and kissed him, and wrote letters for him unto all the treasurers and lieutenants and captains and governors, that they should safely convey on their way both him, and all those that go up with him to build Jerusalem. He wrote letters also unto the lieutenants that were in

Letters of Darius

Celosyria and Phenice, and unto them in Libanus, that they should bring cedar wood from Libanus unto Jerusalem, and that they should build the city with him. Moreover he wrote for all the Jews that went out of his realm up into Jewry, concerning their freedom, that no officer, no ruler, no lieutenant, nor treasurer, should forcibly enter into their doors; and that all the country which they hold should be free without tribute; and that the Edomite, should give over the villages of the Jews which then they held: yea, that there should be yearly given twenty talents to the building of the temple, until the time that it were built; and other ten talents yearly, to maintain the burnt offerings upon the altar every day, as they had a commandment to offer seventeen: and that all they that went from Babylon to build the city should have free liberty, as well they as their posterity, and all the priests that went away. He wrote also concerning the charges, and the priests' vestments wherein they minister; and likewise for the charges of the Levites, to be given them until the day that the house were finished, and Jerusalem builded up. And he commanded to give to all that kept the city pensions and wages. He sent away also all the vessels from Babylon, that Cyrus had set apart; and all that Cyrus had given in commandment, the same charged he also to be done, and sent unto Jerusalem.

Now when this young man was gone forth, he

Prayer of the Young Man

lifted up his face to heaven toward Jerusalem, and praised the King of heaven, and said, From thee cometh victory, from thee cometh wisdom, and thine is the glory, and I am thy servant. Blessed art thou, who hast given me wisdom: for to thee I give thanks, O Lord of our fathers. And so he took the letters, and went out, and came unto Babylon, and told it all his brethren. And they praised the God of their fathers, because he had given them freedom and liberty to go up, and to build Jerusalem, and the temple which is called by his name: and they feasted with instruments of musick and gladness seven days.

* After this were the principal men of the families chosen according to their tribes, to go up with their wives and sons and daughters, with their menservants and maidservants, and their cattle. And Darius sent with them a thousand horsemen, till they had brought them back to Jerusalem safely, and with musical [instruments] tabrets and flutes. And all their brethren played, and he made them go up together with them.

And these are the names of the men which went up, according to their families among their tribes, after their several heads. The priests, the sons of Phinees the son of Aaron: Jesus the son of Josedec, the son of Seraias, and Joacim the son of Zorobabel, the son of Salathiel, of the house of David, out of the kindred of Phares, of the tribe of Judah; who spake wise sentences before Darius the king of Persia in the second year of his reign, in the month Nisan, which is the first month.

Those w returned from Exi

And these are they of Jewry that came up from the captivity, where they dwelt as strangers, whom Nabuchodonosor the king of Babylon had carried away unto Babylon. And they returned unto Jerusalem, and to the other parts of Jewry, every man to his own city, who came with Zorobabel, with Jesus, Nehemias, and Zacharias, and Reesaias, Enenius, Mardocheus, Beelsarus, Aspharasus, Reelius, Roimus, and Baana, their guides. The number of them of the nation, and their governors, sons of Phoros, two thousand an hundred seventy and two: the sons of Saphat, four hundred seventy and two: the sons of Ares, seven hundred fifty and six: the sons of Phaath Moab, two thousand eight hundred and twelve: the sons of Elam, a thousand two hundred fifty and four: the sons of Zathui, nine hundred forty and five: the sons of Corbe, seven hundred and five: the sons of Bani, six hundred forty and eight: the sons of Bebai, six hundred twenty and three: the sons of Sadas, three thousand two hundred twenty and two: the sons of Adonikam, six hundred sixty and seven: the sons of Bagoi, two thousand sixty and six: the sons of Adin, four hundred fifty and four: the sons of Aterezias, ninety and two: the sons of Ceilan and Azetas, threescore and seven: the sons of Azuran, four hundred thirty and two:

Those who returned from Exile

the sons of Ananias, an hundred and one: the sons of Arom, thirty two: and the sons of Bassa, three hundred twenty and three: the sons of Azephurith, an hundred and two: the sons of Meterus, three thousand and five: the sons of Bethlomon, an hundred twenty and three: they of Netophah, fifty and five: they of Anathoth, an hundred fifty and eight: they of Bethsamos, forty and two: they of Kiriathiarius, twenty and five: they of Caphira and Beroth, seven hundred forty and three: they of Pira, seven hundred: they of Chadias and Ammidoi, four hundred twenty and two: they of Cirama and Gabdes, six hundred twenty and one: they of Macalon, an hundred twenty and two: they of Betolius, fifty and two: the sons of Nephis, an hundred fifty and six: the sons of Calamolalus and Onus, seven hundred twenty and five: the sons of Jerechus, two hundred forty and five: the sons of Annaas, three thousand three hundred and thirty.

The priests: the sons of Jeddu, the son of Jesus, among the sons of Sanasib, nine hundred seventy and two: the sons of Meruth, a thousand fifty and two: the sons of Phassaron, a thousand forty and seven: the sons of Carme, a thousand and seventeen.

The Levites: the sons of Jessue, and Cadmiel, and Banuas, and Sudias, seventy and four.

The holy singers: the sons of Asaph, an hundred twenty and eight.

The porters: the sons of Salum, the sons of Jatal,

Those who returned from Exile

the sons of Talmon, the sons of Dacobi, the sons of Teta, the sons of Sami, in all an hundred thirty and nine.

The servants of the temple: the sons of Esau, the sons of Asipha, the sons of Tabaoth, the sons of Ceras, the sons of Sud, the sons of Phaleas, the sons of Labana, the sons of Graba, the sons of Acua, the sons of Uta, the sons of Cetab, the sons of Agaba, the sons of Subai, the sons of Anan, the sons of Cathua, the sons of Geddur, the sons of Airus, the sons of Daisan, the sons of Noeba, the sons of Chaseba, the sons of Gazera, the sons of Azia, the sons of Phinees, the sons of Azara, the sons of Bastai, the sons of Asana, the sons of Meani, the sons of Naphisi, the sons of Acub, the sons of Acipha, the sons of Assur, the sons of Pharacim, the sons of Basaloth, the sons of Meeda, the sons of Coutha, the sons of Charea, the sons of Charcus, the sons of Aserer, the sons of Thomoi, the sons of Nasith, the sons of Atipha.

The sons of the servants of Solomon: the sons of Azaphion, the sons of Pharira, the sons of Jeeli, the sons of Lozon, the sons of Isdael, the sons of Sapheth, the sons of Hagia, the sons of Phacareth, the sons of Sabi, the sons of Sarothie, the sons of Masias, the sons of Gar, the sons of Addus, the sons of Suba, the sons of Apherra, the sons of Barodis, the sons of Sabat, the sons of Allom.

All the ministers of the temple, and the sons of the

The Number of those who returned

servants of Solomon, were three hundred seventy and two. These came up from Thermeleth and Thelersas, Charaathalar leading them, and Aalar; neither could they shew their families, nor their stock, how they were of Israel: the sons of Ladan, the son of Ban, the sons of Necodan, six hundred fifty and two.

And of the priests that usurped the office of the priesthood, and were not found: the sons of Obdia, the son of Accoz, the sons of Addus, who married Augia one of the daughters of Berzelus, and was named after his name. And when the description of the kindred of these men was sought in the register, and was not found, they were removed from executing the office of the priesthood: for unto them said Nehemias and Atharias, that they should not be partakers of the holy things, till there arose up an high priest clothed with doctrine and truth.

So of Israel, from them of twelve years old and upward, they were all in number forty thousand, beside menservants and womenservants two thousand three hundred and sixty. Their menservants and handmaids were seven thousand three hundred forty and seven: the singing men and singing women, two hundred forty and five: four hundred thirty and five camels, seven thousand thirty and six horses, two hundred forty and five mules, five thousand five hundred twenty and five beasts used to the yoke. And certain of the chief of their families, when they came to the temple of God that is in Jerusalem,

The Re-erection o the Altar

vowed to set up the house again in his own place according to their ability, and to give into the holy treasury of the works a thousand pounds of gold, five thousand of silver, and an hundred priestly vestments. And so dwelt the priests and the Levites and the people in Jerusalem, and in the country, the singers also and the porters; and all Israel in their villages.

But when the seventh month was at hand, and when the children of Israel were every man in his own place, they came all together with one consent into the open place of the first gate which is toward the east. Then stood up Jesus the son of Josedec, and his brethren the priests, and Zorobabel the son of Salathiel, and his brethren, and made ready the altar of the God of Israel, to offer burnt sacrifices upon it, according as it is expressly commanded in the book of Moses the man of God.

And there were gathered unto them out of the other nations of the land, and they erected the altar upon his own place, because all the nations of the land were at enmity with them, and oppressed them; and they offered sacrifices according to the time, and burnt offerings to the Lord both morning and evening. Also they held the feast of tabernacles, as it is commanded in the law, and *offered* sacrifices daily, as was meet: and after that, the continual oblations, and the sacrifice of the sabbaths, and of the new moons, and of all holy feasts. And all they that had made any vow to God began to offer sacrifices to God from the first day of

Building of the Second Temple

the seventh month, although the temple of the Lord was not yet built.

And they gave unto the masons and carpenters money, meat, and drink, with cheerfulness. Unto them of Zidon also and Tyre they gave carrs, that they should bring cedar trees from Libanus, which should be brought by floats to the haven of Joppe, according as it was commanded them by Cyrus king of the Persians. And in the second year and second month after his coming to the temple of God at Jerusalem began Zorobabel the son of Salathiel, and Jesus the son of Josedec, and their brethren, and the priests, and the Levites, and all they that were come unto Jerusalem out of the captivity: and they laid the foundation of the house of God in the first day of the second month, in the second year after they were come to Jewry and Jerusalem.

And they appointed the Levites from twenty years old over the works of the Lord. Then stood up Jesus, and his sons and brethren, and Cadmiel his brother, and the sons of Madiabun, with the sons of Joda the son of Eliadun, with their sons and brethren, all Levites, with one accord setters forward of the business, labouring to advance the works in the house of God. So the workmen built the temple of the Lord. And the priests stood arrayed in their vestments with musical instruments and trumpets; and the Levites the sons of Asaph had cymbals, singing songs of thanksgiving, and

Building of the Second Temple

praising the Lord, according as David the king of Israel had ordained. And they sung *with* loud voices songs to the praise of the Lord, because his mercy and glory is for ever in all Israel.

And all the people sounded trumpets, and shouted with a loud voice, singing songs of thanksgiving unto the Lord for the rearing up of the house of the Lord. Also of the priests and Levites, and of the chief of their families, the ancients who had seen the former house came to the building of this with weeping and great crying. But many with trumpets and joy shouted with loud voice, insomuch that the trumpets might not be heard for the weeping of the people: yet the multitude sounded marvellously, so that it was heard afar off.

Wherefore when the enemies of the tribe of Judah and Benjamin heard it, they came to know what that noise of trumpets should mean. And they perceived that they that were of the captivity did build the temple unto the Lord God of Israel. So they went to Zorobabel and Jesus, and to the chief of the families, and said unto them, We will build together with you. For we likewise, as ye, do obey your Lord, and do sacrifice unto him from the days of Azbazareth the king of the Assyrians, who brought us hither.

Then Zorobabel and Jesus and the chief of the families of Israel said unto them, It is not for us and you to build together an house unto the Lord

Enemies attempt to stop the Work

our God. We ourselves alone will build unto the Lord of Israel, according as Cyrus the king of the Persians hath commanded us. But the heathen of the land lying heavy upon the inhabitants of Judea, and holding them strait, hindered their building, and by their secret plots, and popular persuasions and commotions, they hindered the finishing of the building all the time that king Cyrus lived: so they were hindered from building for the space of two years, until the reign of Darius.

* Now in the second year of the reign of Darius Aggeus and Zacharias the son of Addo, the prophets, prophesied unto the Jews in Jewry and Jerusalem in the name of the Lord God of Israel, which was upon them. Then stood up Zorobabel the son of Salathiel, and Jesus the son of Josedec, and began to build the house of the Lord at Jerusalem, the prophets of the Lord being with them, *and* helping them. At the same time came unto them Sisinnes the governor of Syria and Phenice, with Sathrabuzanes and his companions, and said unto them, by whose appointment do ye build this house and this roof, and perform all the other things? and who are the workmen that perform these things? Nevertheless the elders of the Jews obtained favour, because the Lord had visited the captivity; and they were not hindered from building, until such time as signification was given unto Darius concerning them, and an answer received.

The Letter of Sisinnes

The copy of the letters which Sisinnes, governor of Syria and Phenice, and Sathrabuzanes, with their companions, rulers in Syria and Phenice, wrote and sent unto Darius; To king Darius, greeting: Let all things be known unto our lord the king, that being come into the country of Judea, and entered into the city of Jerusalem, we found in the city of Jerusalem the ancients of the Jews that were of the captivity building an house unto the Lord, great *and* new, of hewn and costly stones, and the timber already laid upon the walls. And those works are done with great speed, and the work goeth on prosperously in their hands, and with all glory and diligence is it made. Then asked we these elders, saying, By whose commandment build ye this house, and lay the foundations of these works? Therefore to the intent that we might give knowledge unto thee by writing, we demanded of them who were the chief doers, and we required of them the names in writing of their principal men. So they gave us this answer, We are the servants of the Lord which made heaven and earth. And as for this house, it was builded many years ago by a king of Israel great and strong, and was finished. But when our fathers provoked God unto wrath, and sinned against the Lord of Israel which is in heaven, he gave them over into the power of Nabuchodonosor king of Babylon, of the Chaldees; who pulled down the house, and burned it, and carried away the people captives unto Babylon. But

Darius searches the Records

in the first year that king Cyrus reigned over the country of Babylon Cyrus the king wrote to build up this house. And the holy vessels of gold and of silver, that Nabuchodonosor had carried away out of the house at Jerusalem, and had set them in his own temple, those Cyrus the king brought forth again out of the temple at Babylon, and they were delivered to Zorobabel and to Sanabassarus the ruler, with commandment that he should carry away the same vessels, and put them in the temple at Jerusalem; and that the temple of the Lord should be built in his place. Then the same Sanabassarus, being come hither, laid the foundations of the house of the Lord at Jerusalem; and from that time to this being still a building, it is not yet fully ended. Now therefore, if it seem good unto the king, let search be made among the records of king Cyrus: and if it be found that the building of the house of the Lord at Jerusalem hath been done with the consent of king Cyrus, and if our lord the king be so minded, let him signify unto us thereof.

Then commanded king Darius to seek among the records at Babylon: and so at Ecbatana the palace, which is in the country of Media, there was found a roll wherein these things were recorded. In the first year of the reign of Cyrus king Cyrus commanded that the house of the Lord at Jerusalem should be built again, where they do sacrifice with continual fire: whose height shall be sixty cubits, and the breadth sixty cubits, with three rows of hewn stones,

Confirms Decree fo building the Temp

and one row of new wood of that country; and the expences thereof to be given out of the house of king Cyrus: and that the holy vessels of the house of the Lord, both of gold and silver, that Nabuchodonosor took out of the house at Jerusalem, and brought to Babylon, should be restored to the house at Jerusalem, and be set in the place where they were before. And also he commanded that Sisinnes the governor of Syria and Phenice, and Sathrabuzanes, and their companions, and those which were appointed rulers in Syria and Phenice, should be careful not to meddle with the place, but suffer Zorobabel, the servant of the Lord and governor of Judea, and the elders of the Jews, to build the house of the Lord in that place. I have commanded also to have it built up whole again; and that they look diligently to help those that be of the captivity of the Jews, till the house of the Lord be finished: and out of the tribute of Celosyria and Phenice a portion carefully to be given these men for the sacrifices of the Lord, *that is*, to Zorobabel the governor, for bullocks, and rams, and lambs; and also corn, salt, wine, and oil, and that continually every year without further question, according as the priests that be in Jerusalem shall signify to be daily spent: that offerings may be made to the Most High God for the king and for his children, and that they may pray for their lives. And he commanded that whosoever should transgress, yea, or make light of any thing afore spoken or written, out

Completion of the Temple

of his own house should a tree be taken, and he thereon be hanged, and all his goods seized for the king. The Lord therefore, whose name is there called upon, utterly destroy every king and nation, that stretcheth out his hand to hinder or endamage that house of the Lord in Jerusalem. I Darius the king have ordained that according unto these things it be done with diligence.

* Then Sisinnes the governor of Celosyria and Phenice, and Sathrabuzanes, with their companions, following the commandments of king Darius, did very carefully oversee the holy works, assisting the ancients of the Jews and governors of the temple. And so the holy works prospered, when Aggeus and Zacharias the prophets prophesied. And they finished these things by the commandment of the Lord God of Israel, and with the consent of Cyrus, Darius, and Artaxerxes, kings of Persia. And thus was the holy house finished in the three and twentieth day of the month Adar, in the sixth year of Darius king of the Persians.

And the children of Israel, the priests, and the Levites, and others that were of the captivity, that were added unto them, did according to the things written in the book of Moses. And to the dedication of the temple of the Lord they offered an hundred bullocks, two hundred rams, four hundred lambs; and twelve goats for the sin of all Israel, according to the number of the chief of the tribes of

Dedicatio of the Temple

Israel. The priests also and the Levites stood arrayed in their vestments, according to their kindreds, in the service of the Lord God of Israel, according to the book of Moses: and the porters at every gate.

And the children of Israel that were of the captivity held the passover the fourteenth day of the first month, after that the priests and the Levites were sanctified. They that were of the captivity were not all sanctified together: but the Levites were all sanctified together. And so they offered the passover for all them of the captivity, and for their brethren the priests, and for themselves. And the children of Israel that came out of the captivity did eat, even all they that had separated themselves from the abominations of the people of the land, and sought the Lord. And they kept the feast of unleavened bread seven days, making merry before the Lord, for that he had turned the counsel of the king of Assyria toward them, to strengthen their hands in the works of the Lord God of Israel.

* And after these things, when Artaxerxes the king of the Persians reigned, came Esdras the son of Saraias, the son of Ezerias, the son of Helchiah, the son of Salum, the son of Sadduc, the son of Achitob, the son of Amarias, the son of Ezias, the son of Meremoth, the son of Zaraias, the son of Savias, the son of Boccas, the son of Abisum, the son of Phinees, the son of Eleazar, the son of Aaron the chief priest.

The Character of Esdras

This Esdras went up from Babylon, as a scribe, being very ready in the law of Moses, that was given by the God of Israel. And the king did him honour: for he found grace in his sight in all his requests. There went up with him also certain of the children of Israel, of the priests, of the Levites, of the holy singers, porters, and ministers of the temple, unto Jerusalem, in the seventh year of the reign of Artaxerxes, in the fifth month, this was the king's seventh year; for they went from Babylon in the first day of the first month, and came to Jerusalem, according to the prosperous journey which the Lord gave them. For Esdras had very great skill, so that he omitted nothing of the law and commandments of the Lord, but taught all Israel the ordinances and judgments.

Now the copy of the commission, which was written from Artaxerxes the king, and came to Esdras the priest and reader of the law of the Lord, is this that followeth; King Artaxerxes unto Esdras the priest and reader of the law of the Lord sendeth greeting: Having determined to deal graciously, I have given order, that such of the nation of the Jews, and of the priests and Levites, being within our realm, as are willing and desirous, should go with thee unto Jerusalem. As many therefore as have a mind thereunto, let them depart with thee, as it hath seemed good both to me and my seven friends the counsellors; that they may look unto the affairs of

Commission o Esdras

Judea and Jerusalem, agreeably to that which is in the law of the Lord; and carry the gifts unto the Lord of Israel to Jerusalem, which I and my friends have vowed, and all the gold and silver that in the country of Babylon can be found, to the Lord in Jerusalem, with that also which is given of the people for the temple of the Lord their God at Jerusalem: and that silver and gold may be collected for bullocks, rams, and lambs, and things thereunto appertaining; to the end that they may offer sacrifices unto the Lord upon the altar of the Lord their God, which is in Jerusalem. And whatsoever thou and thy brethren will do with the silver and gold, that do, according to the will of thy God. And the holy vessels of the Lord, which are given thee for the use of the temple of thy God, which is in Jerusalem, thou shalt set before thy God in Jerusalem. And whatsoever thing else thou shalt remember for the use of the temple of thy God, thou shalt give it out of the king's treasury. And I king Artaxerxes have also commanded the keepers of the treasures in Syria and Phenice, that whatsoever Esdras the priest and the reader of the law of the Most High God shall send for, they should give it him with speed, to the sum of an hundred talents of silver, likewise also of wheat even to an hundred cors, and an hundred pieces of wine, and other things in abundance. Let all things be performed after the law of God diligently unto the Most High God, that wrath come not upon the

Commission of Esdras

kingdom of the king and his sons. I command you also, that ye require no tax, nor any other imposition, of any of the priests, or Levites, or holy singers, or porters, or ministers of the temple, or of any that have doings in this temple, and that no man have authority to impose any thing upon them. And thou, Esdras, according to the wisdom of God ordain judges and justices, that they may judge in all Syria and Phenice all those that know the law of thy God; and those that know it not thou shalt teach. And whosoever shall transgress the law of thy God, and of the king, shall be punished diligently, whether it be by death, or other punishment, by penalty of money, or by imprisonment.

Then said Esdras the scribe, Blessed be the only Lord God of my fathers, who hath put these things into the heart of the king, to glorify his house that is in Jerusalem: and hath honoured me in the sight of the king, and his counsellors, and all his friends and nobles. Therefore was I encouraged by the help of the Lord my God, and gathered together men of Israel to go up with me. And these are the chief according to their families and several dignities, that went up with me from Babylon in the reign of king Artaxerxes:

Of the sons of Phinees, Gerson: of the sons of Ithamar, Gamael: of the sons of David, Lettus the son of Sechenias: of the sons of Pharez, Zacharias; and with him were counted an hundred and fifty

Chief Men who accompanied Esdras

men: of the sons of Pahath Moab, Eliaonias, the son or Zaraias, and with him two hundred men: of the sons of Zathoe, Sechenias the son of Jezelus, and with him three hundred men: of the sons of Adin, Oheth the son of Jonathan, and with him two hundred and fifty men: of the sons of Elam, Josias son of Gotholias, and with him seventy men: of the sons of Saphatias, Zaraias son of Michael, and with him threescore and ten men: of the sons of Joab, Abadias son of Jezelus, and with him two hundred and twelve men: of the sons of Banid, Assalimoth son of Josaphias, and with him an hundred and threescore men: of the sons of Babi, Zacharias son of Bebai, and with him twenty and eight men: of the sons of Astath, Johannes *son of* Acatan, and with him an hundred and ten men: of the sons of Adonikam the last, and these are the names of them, Eliphalet, Jeuel, and Samaias, and with them seventy men: of the sons of Bago, Uthi the son of Istalcurus, and with him seventy men.

And these I gathered together to the river called Theras, where we pitched our tents three days: and then I surveyed them. But when I had found there none of the priests and Levites, then sent I unto Eleazar, and Iduel, and Masman, and Alnathan, and Mamaias, and Joribas, and Nathan, Eunatan, Zacharias, and Mosollamon, principal men and learned. And I bade them that they should go unto Saddeus the captain, who was in the place of

The Fast decreed

the treasury: and commanded them that they should speak unto Daddeus, and to his brethren, and to the treasurers in that place, to send as such men as might execute the priests' office in the house of the Lord. And by the mighty hand of our Lord they brought unto us skilful men of the sons of Moli the son of Levi, the son of Israel, Asebebia, and his sons, and his brethren, who were eighteen. And Asebia, and Annuus, and Osaias his brother, of the sons of Channuneus, and their sons, were twenty men. And of the servants of the temple whom David had ordained, and the principal men for the service of the Levites, to wit, the servants of the temple, two hundred and twenty, the catalogue of whose names were shewed.

And there I vowed a fast unto the young men before our Lord, to desire of him a prosperous journey both for us and them that were with us, for our children, and for the cattle: for I was ashamed to ask the king footmen, and horsemen, and conduct for safeguard against our adversaries. For we had said unto the king, that the power of the Lord our God should be with them that seek him, to support them in all ways. And again we besought our Lord as touching these things, and found him favourable unto us.

Then I separated twelve of the chief of the priests, Esebrias, and Assanias, and ten men of their brethren with them: and I weighed them the gold,

Esdras arrives in Jerusalem

and the silver, and the holy vessels of the house of our Lord, which the king, and his council, and the princes, and all Israel, had given. And when I had weighed it, I delivered unto them six hundred and fifty talents of silver, and silver vessels of an hundred talents, and an hundred talents of gold, and twenty golden vessels, and twelve vessels of brass, even of fine brass, glittering like gold.

And I said unto them, Both ye are holy unto the Lord, and the vessels are holy, and the gold and the silver is a vow unto the Lord, the Lord of our fathers. Watch ye, and keep them till ye deliver them to the chief of the priests and Levites, and to the principal men of the families of Israel in Jerusalem, into the chambers of the house of our God. So the priests and the Levites, who had received the silver and the gold and the vessels, brought them unto Jerusalem, into the temple of the Lord.

And from the river Theras we departed the twelfth day of the first month, and came to Jerusalem by the mighty hand of our Lord, which was with us: and from the beginning of our journey the Lord delivered us from every enemy, and *so* we came to Jerusalem. And when we had been there three days, the gold and silver that was weighed was delivered in the house of our Lord on the fourth day unto Marmoth the priest the son of Iri. And with him was Eleazar the son of Phinees, and with them were Josabad the son of Jesu and Moeth the son of

Inter-marriage with Idolaters

Sabban, Levites: all was *delivered them* by number and weight. And all the weight of them was written up the same hour. Moreover they that were come out of the captivity offered sacrifice unto the Lord God of Israel, even twelve bullocks for all Israel, fourscore and sixteen rams, threescore and twelve lambs, goats for a peace offering, twelve; all of them a sacrifice to the Lord. And they delivered the king's commandments unto the king's stewards, and to the governors of Celosyria and Phenice; and they honoured the people and the temple of God.

Now when these things were done, the rulers came unto me, and said, The nation of Israel, the princes, the priests and Levites, have not put away from them the strange people of the land, nor the pollutions of the Gentiles, *to wit*, of the Canaanites, Hittites, Pheresites, Jebusites, and the Moabites, Egyptians, and Edomites. For both they and their sons have married with their daughters, and the holy seed is mixed with the strange people of the land; and from the beginning of this matter the rulers and the great men have been partakers of this iniquity. And as soon as I had heard these things, I rent my clothes, and the holy garment, and pulled off the hair from off my head and beard, and sat me down sad and very heavy. So all they that were then moved at the word of the Lord God of Israel assembled unto me, whilst I mourned for the ini-

Prayer of Esdras

quity: but I sat still full of heaviness until the evening sacrifice. Then rising up from the fast with my clothes and the holy garment rent, and bowing my knees, and stretching forth my hands unto the Lord, I said,

O Lord, I am confounded and ashamed before thy face; for our sins are multiplied above our heads, and our ignorances have reached up unto heaven. For ever since the time of our fathers we *have been* and are in great sin, even unto this day. And for our sins and our fathers' we with our brethren and our kings and our priests were given up unto the kings of the earth, to the sword, and to captivity, and for a prey with shame, unto this day. And now in some measure hath mercy been shewed unto us from thee, O Lord, that there should be left us a root and a name in the place of thy sanctuary; and to discover unto us a light in the house of the Lord our God, and to give us food in the time of our servitude. Yea, when we were in bondage, we were not forsaken of our Lord; but he made us gracious before the kings of Persia, so that they gave us food; yea, and honoured the temple of our Lord, and raised up the desolate Sion, that they have given us a sure abiding in Jewry and Jerusalem. And now, O Lord, what shall we say, having these things? for we have transgressed thy commandments, which thou gavest by the hand of thy servants the prophets, saying, that the land, which ye enter into to possess as an

Prayer of Esdras

heritage, is a land polluted with the pollutions of the strangers of the land, and they have filled it with their uncleanness. Therefore now shall ye not join your daughters unto their sons, neither shall ye take their daughters unto your sons. Moreover ye shall never seek to have peace with them, that ye may be strong, and eat the good things of the land, and that ye may leave the inheritance of the land unto your children for evermore. And all that is befallen is done unto us for our wicked works and great sins: for thou, O Lord, didst make our sins light, and didst give unto us such a root: but we have turned back again to transgress thy law, and to mingle ourselves with the uncleanness of the nations of the land. Mightest not thou be angry with us to destroy us, till thou hadst left us neither root, seed, nor name? O Lord of Israel, thou art true: for we are left a root this day. Behold, now are we before thee in our iniquities, for we cannot stand any longer by reason of these things before thee.

And as Esdras in his prayer made his confession, weeping, and lying flat upon the ground before the temple, there gathered unto him from Jerusalem a very great multitude of men and women and children: for there was great weeping among the multitude. Then Jechonias the son of Jeelus, one of the sons of Israel, called out, and said, O Esdras, we have sinned against the Lord God, we have married strange women of the nations of the land, and now is all Israel

Vow to divorce Heathen Wives

aloft. Let us make an oath to the Lord, that we will put away all our wives, which we have taken of the heathen, with their children, like as thou hast decreed, and as many as do obey the law of the Lord. Arise, and put in execution: for to thee doth this matter appertain, and we will be with thee: do valiantly.

So Esdras arose, and took an oath of the chief of the priests and Levites of all Israel to do after these things; and *so* they sware.

* Then Esdras rising from the court of the temple went to the chamber of Joanan the son of Eliasib, and remained there, and did eat no meat nor drink water, mourning for the great iniquities of the multitude. And there was a proclamation in all Jewry and Jerusalem to all them that were of the captivity, that they should be gathered together at Jerusalem: and that whosoever met not there within two or three days, according as the elders that bare rule appointed, their cattle should be seized to the use of the temple, and himself cast out from them that were of the captivity.

And in three days were all they of the tribe of Judah and Benjamin gathered together at Jerusalem the twentieth day of the ninth month. And all the multitude sat trembling in the broad court of the temple because of the present foul weather. So Esdras arose up, and said unto them, Ye have transgressed the law in marrying strange wives, thereby to

Those who had intermarried

increase the sins of Israel. And now by confessing give glory unto the Lord God of our fathers, and do his will, and separate yourselves from the heathen of the land, and from the strange women.

Then cried the whole multitude, and said with a loud voice, Like as thou hast spoken, so will we do. But forasmuch as the people are many, and it is foul weather, so that we cannot stand without, and this is not a work of a day or two, seeing our sin in these things is spread far: therefore let the rulers of the multitude stay, and let all them of our habitations that have strange wives come at the time appointed, and with them the rulers and judges of every place, till we turn away the wrath of the Lord from us for this matter. Then Jonathan the son of Azael and Ezechias the son of Theocanus accordingly took this matter upon them: and Mosollam and Levis and Sabbatheus helped them. And they that were of the captivity did according to all these things.

And Esdras the priest chose unto him the principal men of their families, all by name: and in the first day of the tenth month they sat together to examine the matter. So their cause that held strange wives was brought to an end in the first day of the first month. And of the priests that were come together, and had strange wives, there were found; of the sons of Jesus the son of Josedec, and his brethren; Matthelas, and Eleazar, and Joribus, and Joadanus. And they gave their hands to put away their wives,

Those w had inter married

and to offer rams to make reconcilement for their errors.

And of the sons of Emmer; Ananias, and Zabdeus, and Eanes, and Sameius, and Hiereel, and Azarias. And of the sons of Phaisur; Elionas, Massias, Ismael, and Nathanael, and Ocidelus, and Talsas. And of the Levites; Jozabad, and Semis, and Colius, who was called Calitas, and Patheus, and Judas, and Jonas. Of the holy singers; Eleazurus, Bacchurus. Of the porters; Sallumus, and Tolbanes. Of them of Israel, of the sons of Phoros; Hiermas, and Eddias, and Melchias, and Maelus, and Eleazar, and Asibias, and Baanias. Of the sons of Ela; Matthanias, Zacharias, and Hierielus, and Hieremoth, and Aedias. And of the sons of Zamoth; Eliadas, Elisimus, Othonias, Jarimoth, and Sabatus, and Sardeus. Of the sons of Bebai; Johannes, and Ananias, and Josabad, and Amatheis. Of the sons of Mani; Olamus, Mamuchus, Jedeus, Jasubus, Jasael, and Hieremoth. And of the sons of Addi; Naathus, and Moosias, Lacunus, and Naidus, and Mathanias, and Sesthel, Balnuus, and Manasseas. And of the sons of Annas; Elionas, and Aseas, and Melchias, and Sabbeus, and Simon Chosameus. And of the sons of Asom; Altaneus, and Matthias, and Bannaia, Eliphalet, and Manasses, and Semei. And of the sons of Maani; Jeremias, Momdis, Omaerus, Juel, Mabdai, and Pelias, and Anos, Carabasion, and Enasibus, and Mamnitanaimus, Eliasis, Bannus, Eliali,

The Law read in Public

Samis, Selemias, Nathanias: and of the sons of Ozora; Sesis, Esril, Azaelus, Samatus, Zambis, Josephus. And of the sons of Ethma; Mazitias, Zabadaias, Edes, Juel, Banaias. All these had taken strange wives, and they put them away with their children.

And the priests and Levites, and they that were of Israel, dwelt in Jerusalem, and in the country, in the first day of the seventh month: so the children of Israel were in their habitations. And the whole multitude came together with one accord into the broad place of the holy porch toward the east: and they spake unto Esdras the priest and reader, that he would bring the law of Moses, that was given of the Lord God of Israel.

So Esdras the chief priest brought the law unto the whole multitude from man to woman, and to all the priests, to hear the law in the first day of the seventh month. And he read in the broad court before the holy porch from morning unto midday, before both men and women; and all the multitude gave heed unto the law. And Esdras the priest and reader of the law stood up upon a pulpit of wood, which was made *for that purpose*. And there stood up by him Mattathias, Sammus, Ananias, Azarias, Urias, Ezecias, Balasamus upon the right hand: and upon his left hand stood Phaldaius, Misael, Melchias, Lothasubus, and Nabarias.

Then took Esdras the book of the law before the

The Law taught to the People

multitude: for he sat honourably in the first place in the sight of them all. And when he opened the law, they stood all straight up. So Esdras blessed the Lord God Most High, the God of hosts, Almighty. And all the people answered, Amen; and lifting up their hands they fell to the ground, and worshipped the Lord. Also Jesus, Anus, Sarabias, Adinus, Jacubus, Sabateas, Auteas, Maianeas, and Calitas, Azarias, and Joazabdus, and Ananias, Biatas, the Levites, taught the law of the Lord, making them withal to understand it.

Then spake Attharates unto Esdras the chief priest and reader, and to the Levites that taught the multitude, even to all, saying, This day is holy unto the Lord; (for they all wept when they heard the law:) go then, and eat the fat, and drink the sweet, and send part to them that have nothing; for this day is holy unto the Lord: and be not sorrowful; for the Lord will bring you to honour.

So the Levites published all things to the people, saying, This day is holy to the Lord; be not sorrowful. Then went they their way, every one to eat and drink, and make merry, and to give part to them that had nothing, and to make great cheer; because they understood the words wherein they were instructed, and for the which they had been assembled.

The Second Book of Esdras

The Word of the Lord to Esdras

THE second book of the prophet Esdras, the son of Saraias, the son of Azarias, the son of Helchias, the son of Sadamias, the son of Sadoc, the son of Achitob, the son of Achias, the son of Phinees, the son of Heli, the son of Amarias, the son of Azici, the son of Marimoth, the son of Arna, the son of Ozias, the son of Borith, the son of Abisei, the son of Phinees, the son of Eleazar, the son of Aaron, of the tribe of Levi; which was captive in the land of the Medes, in the reign of Artaxerxes king of the Persians.

And the word of the Lord came unto me, saying, Go thy way, and shew my people their sinful deeds, and their children their wickedness which they have done against me; that they may tell their children's children: because the sins of their fathers are increased in them: for they have forgotten me, and have offered unto strange gods. Am not I even he that brought them out of the land of Egypt, from the house of bondage? but they have provoked me unto wrath, and despised my counsels. Pull thou off then the hair of thy head, and cast all evil upon them, for they have not been obedient unto my law, but it is a rebellious people. How long shall I forbear them,

The Wor of the Lord to Esdras

unto whom I have done so much good? Many kings have I destroyed for their sakes; Pharaoh with his servants and all his power have I smitten down. All the nations have I destroyed before them, and in the east I have scattered the people of two provinces, even of Tyrus and Sidon, and have slain all their enemies. Speak thou therefore unto them, saying,

Thus saith the Lord, I led you through the sea, and in the beginning gave you a large and safe passage; I gave you Moses for a leader, and Aaron for a priest. I gave you light in a pillar of fire, and great wonders have I done among you; yet have ye forgotten me, saith the Lord. Thus saith the Almighty Lord, The quails were as a token to you; I gave you tents for your safeguard: nevertheless ye murmured there, and triumphed not in my name for the destruction of your enemies, but ever to this day do ye yet murmur. Where are the benefits that I have done for you? when ye were hungry and thirsty in the wilderness, did ye not cry unto me, saying, Why hast thou brought us into this wilderness to kill us? it had been better for us to have served the Egyptians, than to die in this wilderness. Then had I pity upon your mournings, and gave you manna to eat; so ye did eat angels' bread. When ye were thirsty, did I not cleave the rock, and waters flowed out to your fill? for the heat I covered you with the leaves of the trees. I divided among you a fruitful land, I cast out the Canaanites, the Pherezites, and the Philistines, before you: what shall I yet do more for you? saith the Lord.

Thus saith the Almighty Lord, When ye were in the wilderness, in the river of the Amorites, being athirst, and blaspheming my name, I gave you not fire for your blasphemies, but cast a tree in the water, and made the river sweet. What shall I do unto thee, O Jacob? thou, Juda, wouldest not obey me: I will turn me to other nations, and unto those will I give my name, that they may keep my statutes. Seeing ye have forsaken me, I will forsake you also; when ye desire me to be gracious unto you, I shall have no mercy upon you. Whensoever ye shall call upon me, I will not hear you: for ye have defiled your hands with blood, and your feet are swift to commit manslaughter. Ye have not as it were forsaken me, but your own selves, saith the Lord.

Thus saith the Almighty Lord, Have I not prayed you as a father his sons, as a mother her daughters, and a nurse her young babes, that ye would be my people, and I should be your God; that ye would be my children, and I should be your father? I gathered you together, as a hen gathereth her chickens under her wings: but now, what shall I do unto you? I will cast you out from my face. When ye offer unto me, I will turn my face from you: for your solemn feastdays, your new moons, and your circumcisions, have I forsaken. I sent

The Coming Calamities

unto you my servants the prophets, whom ye have taken and slain, and torn their bodies in pieces, whose blood I will require of your hands, saith the Lord.

Thus saith the Almighty Lord, Your house is desolate, I will cast you out as the wind doth stubble.

And your children shall not be fruitful; for they have despised my commandment, and done the thing that is evil before me. Your houses will I give to a people that shall come; which not having heard of me yet shall believe me; to whom I have shewed no signs, yet they shall do that I have commanded them. They have seen no prophets, yet they shall call their sins to remembrance, and acknowledge them. I take to witness the grace of the people to come, whose little ones rejoice in gladness: and though they have not seen me with bodily eyes, yet in spirit they believe the thing that I say.

And now, brother, behold what glory; and see the people that come from the east: unto whom I will give for leaders, Abraham, Isaac, and Jacob, Oseas, Amos, and Micheas, Joel, Abdias, and Jonas, Nahum, and Abacuc, Sophonias, Aggeus, Zachary, and Malachy, which is called also an angel of the Lord.

* Thus saith the Lord, I brought this people out of bondage, and I gave them my commandments by my servants the prophets; whom they would not hear,

The Prophecy of Coming Doom

but despised my counsels. The mother that bare them saith unto them, Go your way, ye children; for I am a widow and forsaken. I brought you up with gladness; but with sorrow and heaviness have I lost you: for ye have sinned before the Lord your God, and done that thing that is evil before him. But what shall I now do unto you? I am a widow and forsaken: go your way, O my children, and ask mercy of the Lord. As for me, O father, I call upon thee for a witness over the mother of these children, which would not keep my covenant. That thou bring them to confusion, and their mother to a spoil, that there may be no offspring of them. Let them be scattered abroad among the heathen, let their names be put out of the earth: for they have despised my covenant. Woe be unto thee, Assur, thou that hidest the unrighteous in thee! O thou wicked people, remember what I did unto Sodom and Gomorrha; whose land lieth in clods of pitch and heaps of ashes: even so also will I do unto them that hear me not, saith the Almighty Lord.

Thus saith the Lord unto Esdras, Tell my people that I will give them the kingdom of Jerusalem, which I would have given unto Israel. Their glory also will I take unto me, and give these the everlasting tabernacles, which I had prepared for them. They shall have the tree of life for an ointment of sweet savour; they shall neither labour, nor be weary. Go, and ye shall receive: pray for few

Kingdom prepared for God's Own

days unto you, that they may be shortened: the kingdom is already prepared for you: watch. Take heaven and earth to witness; for I have broken the evil in pieces, and created the good: for I live, saith the Lord.

Mother, embrace thy children, and bring them up with gladness, make their feet as fast as a pillar: for I have chosen thee, saith the Lord. And those that be dead will I raise up again from their places, and bring them out of the graves: for I have known my name in Israel. Fear not, thou mother of the children: for I have chosen thee, saith the Lord. For thy help will I send my servants Esay and Jeremy, after whose counsel I have sanctified and prepared for thee twelve trees laden with divers fruits, and as many fountains flowing with milk and honey, and seven mighty mountains, whereupon there grow roses and lilies, whereby I will fill thy children with joy. Do right to the widow, judge for the fatherless, give to the poor, defend the orphan, clothe the naked, heal the broken and the weak, laugh not a lame man to scorn, defend the maimed, and let the blind man come into the sight of my clearness. Keep the old and young within thy walls. Wheresoever thou findest the dead, take them and bury them, and I will give thee the first place in my resurrection. Abide still, O my people, and take thy rest, for thy quietness shall come.

Nourish thy children, O thou good nurse; stablish

Esdras receives his Charge

their feet. As for the servants whom I have given thee, there shall not one of them perish; for I will require them from among thy number. Be not weary: for when the day of trouble and heaviness cometh, others shall weep and be sorrowful, but thou shalt be merry and have abundance. The heathen shall envy thee, but they shall be able to do nothing against thee, saith the Lord. My hands shall cover thee, so that thy children shall not see hell. Be joyful, O thou mother, with thy children; for I will deliver thee, saith the Lord. Remember thy children that sleep, for I shall bring them out of the sides of the earth, and shew mercy unto them: for I am merciful, saith the Lord Almighty. Embrace thy children until I come and shew mercy unto them: for my wells run over, and my grace shall not fail.

I Esdras received a charge of the Lord upon the mount Oreb, that I should go unto Israel; but when I came unto them, they set me at nought, and despised the commandment of the Lord. And therefore I say unto you, O ye heathen, that hear and understand, look for your Shepherd, he shall give you everlasting rest; for he is nigh at hand, that shall come in the end of the world. Be ready to the reward of the kingdom, for the everlasting light shall shine upon you for evermore. Flee the shadow of this world, receive the joyfulness of your glory: I testify my Saviour openly. O receive the gift that

The Vision o Esdras

is given you, and be glad, giving thanks unto him that hath called you to the heavenly kingdom. Arise up and stand, behold the number of those that be sealed in the feast of the Lord; which are departed from the shadow of the world, and have received glorious garments of the Lord. Take thy number, O Sion, and shut up those of thine that are clothed in white, which have fulfilled the law of the Lord. The number of thy children, whom thou longedst for, is fulfilled: beseech the power of the Lord, that thy people, which have been called from the beginning, may be hallowed.

I Esdras saw upon the mount Zion a great people, whom I could not number, and they all praised the Lord with songs. And in the midst of them there was a young man of a high stature, taller than all the rest, and upon every one of their heads he set crowns, and was more exalted; which I marvelled at greatly. So I asked the angel, and said, Sir, what are these?

He answered and said unto me, These be they that have put off the mortal clothing, and put on the immortal, and have confessed the name of God: now are they crowned, and receive palms.

Then said I unto the angel, What young person is it that crowneth them, and giveth them palms in their hands?

So he answered and said unto me, It is the son of God, whom they have confessed in the world.

The Prayer of Esdras

Then began I greatly to commend them that stood so stiffly for the name of the Lord.

Then the angel said unto me, Go thy way, and tell my people what manner of things, and how great wonders of the Lord thy God, thou hast seen.

* In the thirtieth year after the ruin of the city I was in Babylon, and lay troubled upon my bed, and my thoughts came up over my heart: for I saw the desolation of Sion, and the wealth of them that dwelt at Babylon. And my spirit was sore moved, so that I began to speak words full of fear to the Most High, and said,

O Lord, who bearest rule, thou spakest at the beginning, when thou didst plant the earth, and that thyself alone, and commandedst the people, and gavest a body unto Adam without soul, which was the workmanship of thine hands, and didst breathe into him the breath of life, and he was made living before thee. And thou leddest him into paradise, which thy right hand had planted, before ever the earth came forward. And unto him thou gavest commandment to love thy way: which he transgressed, and immediately thou appointedst death in him and in his generations, of whom came nations, tribes, people, and kindreds, out of number. And every people walked after their own will, and did wonderful things before thee, and despised thy commandments. And again in process of time thou broughtest the flood upon those that dwelt in the world, and destroyedst them. And it came to pass in every of them, that as death was to Adam, so was the flood to these. Nevertheless one of them thou leftest, namely, Noah with his household, of whom came all righteous men. And it happened, that when they that dwelt upon the earth began to multiply, and had gotten them many children, and were a great people, they began again to be more ungodly than the first.

Now when they lived so wickedly before thee, thou didst choose thee a man from among them, whose name was Abraham. Him thou lovedst, and unto him only thou shewedst thy will: and madest an everlasting covenant with him, promising him that thou wouldest never forsake his seed. And unto him thou gavest Isaac, and unto Isaac also thou gavest Jacob and Esau. As for Jacob, thou didst choose him to thee, and put by Esau: and so Jacob became a great multitude. And it came to pass, that when thou leddest his seed out of Egypt, thou broughtest them up to the mount Sinai. And bowing the heavens, thou didst set fast the earth, movedst the whole world, and madest the depths to tremble, and troubledst the men of that age. And thy glory went through four gates, of fire, and of earthquake, and of wind, and of cold; that thou mightest give the law unto the seed of Jacob, and diligence unto the generation of Israel. And yet tookest thou not away from them a wicked heart, that thy law might bring forth fruit in them. For the first Adam bearing a wicked

The Sinfulness of Israel

heart transgressed, and was overcome; and so be all they that are born of him. Thus infirmity was made permanent; and the law (also) in the heart of the people with the malignity of the root; so that the good departed away, and the evil abode still. So the times passed away, and the years were brought to an end: then didst thou raise thee up a servant, called David: whom thou commandedst to build a city unto thy name, and to offer incense and oblations unto thee therein. When this was done many years, then they that inhabited the city forsook thee, and in all things did even as Adam and all his generations had done: for they also had a wicked heart: and so thou gavest thy city over into the hands of thine enemies. Are their deeds then any better that inhabit Babylon, that they should therefore have the dominion over Sion?

For when I came thither, and had seen impieties without number, then my soul saw many evildoers in this thirtieth year, so that my heart failed me. For I have seen how thou sufferest them sinning, and hast spared wicked doers: and hast destroyed thy people, and hast preserved thine enemies, and hast not signified it. I do not remember how this way may be left: are they then of Babylon better than they of Sion? Or is there any other people that knoweth thee beside Israel? or what generation hath so believed thy covenants as Jacob? And yet their reward appeareth not, and their labour hath no fruit:

The Message of Uriel

for I have gone here and there through the heathen, and I see that they flow in wealth, and think not upon thy commandments. Weigh thou therefore our wickedness now in the balance, and their's also that dwell in the world; and so shall thy name no where be found but in Israel. Or when was it that they which dwell upon the earth have not sinned in thy sight? or what people have so kept thy commandments? Thou shalt find that Israel by name hath kept thy precepts; but not the heathen.

* And the angel that was sent unto me, whose name was Uriel, gave me an answer, and said, Thy heart hath gone too far in this world, and thinkest thou to comprehend the way of the Most High?

Then said I, Yea, my lord.

And he answered me, and said, I am sent to show thee three ways, and to set forth three similitudes before thee: whereof if thou canst declare me one, I will shew thee also the way that thou desirest to see, and I shall shew thee from whence the wicked heart cometh.

And I said, Tell on, my lord.

Then said he unto me, Go thy way, weigh me the weight of the fire, or measure me the blast of the wind, or call me again the day that is past.

Then answered I and said, What man is able to do that, that thou shouldest ask such things of me?

And he said unto me, If I should ask thee how great dwellings are in the midst of the sea, or how

Uriel's Appeal to Esdras

many springs are in the beginning of the deep, or how many springs are above the firmament, or which are the outgoings of paradise: peradventure thou wouldest say unto me, I never went down into the deep, nor as yet into hell, neither did I ever climb up into heaven. Nevertheless now have I asked thee but only of the fire and wind, and of the day wherethrough thou hast passed, and of things from which thou canst not be separated, and yet canst thou give me no answer of them.

He said moreover unto me, Thine own things, and such as are grown up with thee, canst thou not know; how should thy vessel then be able to comprehend the way of the Highest, and, the world being now outwardly corrupted, to understand the corruption that is evident in my sight?

Then said I unto him, It were better that we were not at all, than that we should live still in wickedness, and to suffer, and not to know wherefore.

He answered me, and said, I went into a forest into a plain, and the trees took counsel, and said, Come, let us go and make war against the sea, that it may depart away before us, and that we may make us more woods. The floods of the sea also in like manner took counsel, and said, Come, let us go up and subdue the woods of the plain, that there also we may make us another country. The thought of the wood was in vain, for the fire came and consumed it. The thought of the floods of the sea came likewise

Prayer of Esdras for Understanding

to nought, for the sand stood up and stopped them. If thou wert judge now betwixt these two, whom wouldest thou begin to justify? or whom wouldest thou condemn?

I answered and said, Verily it is a foolish thought that they both have devised, for the ground is given unto the wood, and the sea also hath his place to bear his floods.

Then answered he me, and said, Thou hast given a right judgment, but why judgest thou not thyself also? for like as the ground is given unto the wood, and the sea to his floods: even so they that dwell upon the earth may understand nothing but that which is upon the earth: and he that dwelleth above the heavens may only understand the things that are above the height of the heavens.

Then answered I and said, I beseech thee, O Lord, let me have understanding: for it was not my mind to be curious of the high things, but of such as pass by us daily, namely, wherefore Israel is given up as a reproach to the heathen, and for what cause the people whom thou hast loved is given over unto ungodly nations, and why the law of our forefathers is brought to nought, and the written covenants come to none effect, and we pass away out of the world as grasshoppers, and our life is astonishment and fear, and we are not worthy to obtain mercy. What will he then do unto his name whereby we are called? of these things have I asked.

The Unfathomable Nature of God's Being

Then answered he me, and said, The more thou searchest, the more thou shalt marvel; for the world hasteth fast to pass away, and cannot comprehend the things that are promised to the righteous in time to come: for this world is full of unrighteousness and infirmities. But as concerning the things whereof thou askest me, I will tell thee; for the evil is sown, but the destruction thereof is not yet come. If therefore that which is sown be not turned upside down, and if the place where the evil is sown pass not away, then cannot it come that is sown with good. For the grain of evil seed hath been sown in the heart of Adam from the beginning, and how much ungodliness hath it brought up unto this time? and how much shall it yet bring forth until the time of threshing come? ponder now by thyself, how great fruit of wickedness the grain of evil seed hath brought forth. And when the ears shall be cut down, which are without number, how great a floor shall they fill?

Then I answered and said, How, and when shall these things come to pass? wherefore are our years few and evil?

And he answered me, saying, Do not thou hasten above the Most Highest: for thy haste is in vain to be above him, for thou hast much exceeded. Did not the souls also of the righteous ask question of these things in their chambers, saying, How long shall I hope on this fashion? when cometh the fruit of the floor of our reward? and unto these things

The Request of Esdras

Uriel the archangel gave them answer, and said, Even when the number of seeds is filled in you: for he hath weighed the world in the balance. By measure hath he measured the times, and by number hath he numbered the times; and he doth not move nor stir them, until the said measure be fulfilled.

Then answered I and said, O Lord that bearest rule, even we all are full of impiety. And for our sakes peradventure it is that the floors of the righteous are not filled, because of the sins of them that dwell upon the earth.

So he answered me, and said, Go thy way to a woman with child, and ask of her when she hath fulfilled her nine months, if her womb may keep the birth any longer within her.

Then said I, No, Lord, that can she not.

And he said unto me, In the grave the chambers of souls are like the womb of a woman: for like as a woman that travaileth maketh haste to escape the necessity of the travail: even so do these places haste to deliver those things that are committed unto them. From the beginning, look, what thou desirest to see, it shall be shewed thee.

Then answered I and said, If I have found favour in thy sight, and if it be possible, and if I be meet therefore, shew me then whether there be more to come than is past, or more past than is to come. What is past I know, but what is for to come I know not.

Uriel expounds the Similitude

And he said unto me, Stand up upon the right side, and I shall expound the similitude unto thee.

So I stood, and saw, and, behold, an hot burning oven passed by before me: and it happened, that when the flame was gone by I looked, and, behold, the smoke remained still. After this there passed by before me a watery cloud, and sent down much rain with a storm; and when the stormy rain was past, the drops remained still.

Then said he unto me, Consider with thyself; as the rain is more than the drops, and as the fire is greater than the smoke; but the drops and the smoke remain behind: so the quantity which is past did more exceed.

Then I prayed, and said, May I live, thinkest thou, until that time? or what shall happen in those days?

He answered me, and said, As for the tokens whereof thou askest me, I may tell thee of them in part: but as touching thy life, I am not sent to shew thee; for I do not know it. * Nevertheless as concerning the tokens, behold, the days shall come, that they which dwell upon earth shall be taken in a great number, and the way of truth shall be hidden, and the land shall be barren of faith. But iniquity shall be increased above that which now thou seest, or that thou hast heard long ago. And the land, that thou seest now to have root, shalt thou see wasted suddenly. But if the Most High grant thee

Uriel expounds the Similitude

to live, thou shalt see after the third trumpet that the sun shall suddenly shine again in the night, and the moon thrice in the day: and blood shall drop out of the wood, and the stone shall give his voice, and the people shall be troubled: and even he shall rule, whom they look not for that dwell upon the earth, and the fowls shall take their flight away together: and the Sodomitish sea shall cast out fish, and make a noise in the night, which many have not known: but they shall all hear the voice thereof. There shall be a confusion also in many places, and the fire shall be oft sent out again, and the wild beasts shall change their places, and menstruous women shall bring forth monsters: and salt waters shall be found in the sweet, and all friends shall destroy one another; then shall wit hide itself, and understanding withdraw itself into his secret chamber, and shall be sought of many, and yet not be found: then shall unrighteousness and incontinency be multiplied upon earth. One land also shall ask another, and say, Is righteousness that maketh a man righteous gone through thee? And it shall say, No. At the same time shall men hope, but nothing obtain: they shall labour, but their ways shall not prosper. To shew thee such tokens I have leave; and if thou wilt pray again, and weep as now, and fast seven days, thou shalt hear yet greater things.

Then I awaked, and an extreme fearfulness went through all my body, and my mind was troubled, so

What Esdras underwent to regain Understanding

that it fainted. So the angel that was come to talk with me held me, comforted me, and set me up upon my feet. And in the second night it came to pass, that Salathiel the captain of the people came unto me, saying, Where hast thou been? and why is thy countenance so heavy? Knowest thou not that Israel is committed unto thee in the land of their captivity? Up then, and eat bread, and forsake us not, as the shepherd that leaveth his flock in the hands of cruel wolves. Then said I unto him, Go thy ways from me, and come not nigh me. And he heard what I said, and went from me.

And so I fasted seven days, mourning and weeping, like as Uriel the angel commanded me. And after seven days so it was, that the thoughts of my heart were very grievous unto me again, and my soul recovered the spirit of understanding, and I began to talk with the Most High again, and said,

O Lord that bearest rule, of every wood of the earth, and of all the trees thereof, thou hast chosen thee one only vine: and of all lands of the whole world thou hast chosen thee one pit: and of all the flowers thereof one lily: and of all the depths of the sea thou hast filled thee one river: and of all builded cities thou hast hallowed Sion unto thyself: and of all the fowls that are created thou hast named thee one dove: and of all the cattle that are made thou hast provided thee one sheep: and among all the multitudes of people thou hast gotten thee one people:

Esdras troubled for Israel

and unto this people, whom thou lovedst, thou gavest a law, that is approved of all. And now, O Lord, why hast thou given this one people over unto many? and upon the one root hast thou prepared others, and why hast thou scattered thy only one people among many? And they which did gainsay thy promises, and believed not thy covenants, have trodden them down. If thou didst so much hate thy people, yet shouldest thou punish them with thine own hands.

Now when I had spoken these words, the angel that came to me the night afore was sent unto me, and said unto me, Hear me, and I will instruct thee; hearken to the thing that I say, and I shall tell thee more.

And I said, Speak on, my Lord. Then said he unto me, Thou art sore troubled in mind for Israel's sake: lovest thou that people better than he that made them?

And I said, No, Lord: but of very grief have I spoken: for my reins pain me every hour, while I labour to comprehend the way of the Most High, and to seek out part of his judgment.

And he said unto me, Thou canst not.

And I said, Wherefore, Lord? whereunto was I born then? or why was not my mother's womb then my grave, that I might not have seen the travail of Jacob, and the wearisome toil of the stock of Israel?

And he said unto me, Number me the things that are not yet come, gather me together the drops that

Vanity of Human Wisdom

are scattered abroad, make me the flowers green again that are withered, open me the places that are closed, and bring me forth the winds that in them are shut up, shew me the image of a voice: and then I will declare to thee the thing that thou labourest to know.

And I said, O Lord that bearest rule, who may know these things, but he that hath not his dwelling with men? As for me, I am unwise: how may I then speak of these things whereof thou askest me?

Then said he unto me, Like as thou canst do none of these things that I have spoken of, even so canst thou not find out my judgment, or in the end the love that I have promised unto my people.

And I said, Behold, O Lord, yet art thou nigh unto them that be reserved till the end: and what shall they do that have been before me, or we that be now, or they that shall come after us?

And he said unto me, I will liken my judgment unto a ring: like as there is no slackness of the last, even so there is no swiftness of the first.

So I answered and said, Couldest thou not make those that have been made, and be now, and that are for to come, at once; that thou mightest shew thy judgment the sooner?

Then answered he me, and said, The creature may not haste above the maker; neither may the world hold them at once that shall be created therein.

And I said, As thou hast said unto thy servant,

Uriel's Instruction continued

that thou, which givest life to all, hast given life at once to the creature that thou hast created, and the creature bare it: even so it might now also bear them that now be present at once.

And he said unto me, Ask the womb of a woman, and say unto her, If thou bringest forth children, why dost thou it not together, but one after another? pray her therefore to bring forth ten children at once.

And I said, She cannot: but must do it by distance of time.

Then said he unto me, Even so have I given the womb of the earth to those that be sown in it in their times. For like as a young child may not bring forth the things that belong to the aged, even so have I disposed the world which I created.

And I asked, and said, Seeing thou hast now given me the way, I will *proceed to* speak before thee: for our mother, of whom thou hast told me that she is young, draweth now nigh unto age.

He answered me, and said, Ask a woman that beareth children, and she shall tell thee. Say unto her, Wherefore are not they whom thou hast now brought forth like those that were before, but less of stature? And she shall answer thee, They that be born in the strength of youth are of one fashion, and they that are born in the time of age, when the womb faileth, are otherwise. Consider thou therefore also, how that ye are less of stature than those that were before you. And so are they that come after you

The Lord the only Creator

less than ye, as the creatures which now begin to be old, and have passed over the strength of youth.

Then said I, Lord, I beseech thee, if I have found favour in thy sight, shew thy servant by whom thou visitest thy creature.

* And he said unto me, In the beginning, when the earth was made, before the borders of the world stood, or ever the winds blew, before it thundered and lightened, or ever the foundations of paradise were laid, before the fair flowers were seen, or ever the moveable powers were established, before the innumerable multitude of angels were gathered together, or ever the heights of the air were lifted up, before the measures of the firmament were named, or ever the chimneys in Sion were hot, and ere the present years were sought out, and or ever the inventions of them that now sin were turned, before they were sealed that have gathered faith for a treasure: then did I consider these things, and they all were made through me alone, and through none other: by me also they shall be ended, and by none other.

Then answered I and said, What shall be the parting asunder of the times? or when shall be the end of the first, and the beginning of it that followeth?

And he said unto me, From Abraham unto Isaac, when Jacob and Esau were born of him, Jacob's hand held first the heel of Esau. For Esau is the end of the world, and Jacob is the beginning of it

The Mighty Sounding Voice

that followeth. The hand of man is betwixt the heel and the hand: other question, Esdras, ask thou not.

I answered then and said, O Lord that bearest rule, if I have found favour in thy sight, I beseech thee, shew thy servant the end of thy tokens, whereof thou shewedst me part the last night.

So he answered and said unto me, Stand up upon thy feet, and hear a mighty sounding voice. And it shall be as it were a great motion; but the place where thou standest shall not be moved. And therefore when it speaketh be not afraid: for the word is of the end, and the foundation of the earth is understood. And why? because the speech of these things trembleth and is moved: for it knoweth that the end of these things must be changed.

And it happened, that when I had heard it I stood up upon my feet, and hearkened, and, behold, there was a voice that spake, and the sound of it was like the sound of many waters. And it said, Behold, the days come, that I will begin to draw nigh, and to visit them that dwell upon the earth, and will begin to make inquisition of them, what they be that have hurt unjustly with their unrighteousness, and when the affliction of Sion shall be fulfilled; and when the world, that shall begin to vanish away, shall be finished, then will I shew these tokens: the books shall be opened before the firmament, and they shall see all together: and the children of a year old shall

Faith shall flourish

speak with their voices, the women with child shall bring forth untimely children of three or four months old, and they shall live and be raised up. And suddenly shall the sown places appear unsown, the full storehouses shall suddenly be found empty: and the trumpet shall give a sound, which when every man heareth, they shall be suddenly afraid. At that time shall friends fight one against another like enemies, and the earth shall stand in fear with those that dwell therein, the springs of the fountains shall stand still, and in three hours they shall not run. Whosoever remaineth from all these that I have told thee shall escape, and see my salvation, and the end of your world. And the men that are received shall see it, who have not tasted death from their birth: and the heart of the inhabitants shall be changed, and turned into another meaning. For evil shall be put out, and deceit shall be quenched. As for faith, it shall flourish, corruption shall be overcome, and the truth, which hath been so long without fruit, shall be declared.

And when he talked with me, behold, I looked by little and little upon him before whom I stood. And these words said he unto me; I am come to shew thee the time of the night to come. If thou wilt pray yet more, and fast seven days again, I shall tell thee greater things by day than I have heard. For thy voice is heard before the Most High: for the Mighty hath seen thy righteous dealing, he hath

The Times of Creation

seen also thy chastity, which thou hast had ever since thy youth. And therefore hath he sent me to shew thee all these things, and to say unto thee, Be of good comfort, and fear not. And hasten not with the times that are past, to think vain things, that thou mayest not hasten from the latter times.

And it came to pass after this, that I wept again, and fasted seven days in like manner, that I might fulfil the three weeks which he told me. And in the eighth night was my heart vexed within me again, and I began to speak before the Most High. For my spirit was greatly set on fire, and my soul was in distress. And I said,

O Lord, thou spakest from the beginning of the creation, even the first day, and saidst thus; Let heaven and earth be made; and thy word was a perfect work. And then was the spirit, and darkness and silence were on every side; the sound of man's voice was not yet formed. Then commandedst thou a fair light to come forth of thy treasures, that thy work might appear. Upon the second day thou madest the spirit of the firmament, and commandedst it to part asunder, and to make a division betwixt the waters, that the one part might go up, and the other remain beneath. Upon the third day thou didst command that the waters should be gathered in the seventh part of the earth: six parts hast thou dried up, and kept them, to the intent that of these some being planted of God and tilled might serve thee.

The Times of Creation

For as soon as thy word went forth the work was made. For immediately there was great and innumerable fruit, and many and divers pleasures for the taste, and flowers of unchangeable colour, and odours of wonderful smell: and this was done the third day. Upon the fourth day thou commandedst that the sun should shine, and the moon give her light, and the stars should be in order: and gavest them a charge to do service unto man, that was to be made. Upon the fifth day thou saidst unto the seventh part, where the waters were gathered, that it should bring forth living creatures, fowls and fishes: and so it came to pass. For the dumb water and without life brought forth living things at the commandment of God, that all people might praise thy wondrous works. Then didst thou ordain two living creatures, the one thou calledst Enoch, and the other Leviathan; and didst separate the one from the other: for the seventh part, namely, where the water was gathered together, might not hold them both. Unto Enoch thou gavest one part, which was dried up the third day, that he should dwell in the same part, wherein are a thousand hills: but unto Leviathan thou gavest the seventh part, namely, the moist; and hast kept him to be devoured of whom thou wilt, and when. Upon the sixth day thou gavest commandment unto the earth, that before thee it should bring forth beasts, cattle, and creeping things: and after these, Adam also, whom thou

Uriel visits Esdras again

madest lord of all thy creatures: of him come we all, and the people also whom thou hast chosen. All this have I spoken before thee, O Lord, because thou madest the world for our sakes. As for the other people, which also come of Adam, thou hast said that they are nothing, but be like unto spittle: and hast likened the abundance of them unto a drop that falleth from a vessel. And now, O Lord, behold, these heathen, which have ever been reputed as nothing, have begun to be lords over us, and to devour us. But we thy people, whom thou hast called thy firstborn, thy only begotten, and thy fervent lover, are given into their hands. If the world now be made for our sakes, why do we not possess an inheritance with the world? how long shall this endure?

* And when I had made an end of speaking these words, there was sent unto me the angel [Uriel] which had been sent unto me the nights afore:

And he said unto me, Up, Esdras, and hear the words that I am come to tell thee.

And I said, Speak on, my God.

Then said he unto me, The sea is set in a wide place, that it might be deep and great. But put the case the entrance were narrow, and like a river; who then could go into the sea to look upon it, and to rule it? if he went not through the narrow, how could he come into the broad? There is also another thing; A city is builded, and set upon a

The Coming Good v. the Present Evils

broad field, and is full of all good things: the entrance thereof is narrow, and is set in a dangerous place to fall, like as if there were a fire on the right hand, and on the left a deep water: and one only path between them both, even between the fire and the water, *so small* that there could but one man go there at once. If this city now were given unto a man for an inheritance, if he never shall pass the danger set before it, how shall he receive this inheritance?

And I said, It is so, Lord.

Then said he unto me, Even so also is Israel's portion. Because for their sakes I made the world: and when Adam transgressed my statutes, then was decreed that now is done. Then were the entrances of this world made narrow, full of sorrow and travail: they are but few and evil, full of perils, and very painful. For the entrances of the elder world were wide and sure, and brought immortal fruit. If then they that live labour not to enter these strait and vain things, they can never receive those that are laid up for them. Now therefore why disquietest thou thyself, seeing thou art but a corruptible man? and why art thou moved, whereas thou art but mortal? Why hast thou not considered in thy mind this thing that is to come, rather than that which is present?

Then answered I and said, O Lord that bearest rule, thou hast ordained in thy law, that the

No Judge above God

righteous should inherit these things, but that the ungodly should perish. Nevertheless the righteous shall suffer strait things, and hope for wide: for they that have done wickedly have suffered the strait things, and yet shall not see the wide.

And he said unto me, There is no judge above God, and none that hath understanding above the Highest. For there be many that perish in this life, because they despise the law of God that is set before them. For God hath given strait commandment to such as came, what they should do to live, even as they came, and what they should observe to avoid punishment. Nevertheless they were not obedient unto him; but spake against him, and imagined vain things; and deceived themselves by their wicked deeds; and said of the Most High, that he is not; and knew not his ways: but his law have they despised, and denied his covenants; in his statutes have they not been faithful, and have not performed his works. And therefore, Esdras, for the empty are empty things, and for the full are the full things. Behold, the time shall come, that these tokens which I have told thee shall come to pass, and the bride shall appear, and she coming forth shall be seen, that now is withdrawn from the earth. And whosoever is delivered from the foresaid evils shall see my wonders. For my son Jesus shall be revealed with those that be with him, and they that remain shall rejoice within four hundred years.

The End of Sin & Misery

After these years shall my son Christ die, and all men that have life. And the world shall be turned into the old silence seven days, like as in the former judgments: so that no man shall remain. And after seven days the world, that yet awaketh not, shall be raised up, and that shall die that is corrupt. And the earth shall restore those that are asleep in her, and so shall the dust those that dwell in silence, and the secret places shall deliver those souls that were committed unto them. And the Most High shall appear upon the seat of judgment, and misery shall pass away, and the long suffering shall have an end: but judgment only shall remain, truth shall stand, and faith shall wax strong: and the work shall follow, and the reward shall be shewed, and the good deeds shall be of force, and wicked deeds shall bear no rule.

The place of anguish will then be brought to view, while opposite it shall exist the place of peace. The fire of Gehenna shall be revealed, while opposite it shall be seen the gardens of the blest.

To the races that are brought back from the grave shall the Highest thus speak; Behold him whom ye would not accept, whom ye refused to obey, and whose statutes ye contemned.

Behold and see what is before you on the right hand and on the left, here of a truth pleasure and peace, yonder the flames of Gehenna and anguish. Shalt thou speak in that day of reckoning, a day that

Life hereafter fraught with Bliss

hath no light of sun or moon, or stars, no clouds that bring thunder and lightning, no winds nor rain, neither the gloom of night nor the glory of morning, neither summer's heat, nor spring's growth, nor winter's storm, neither frost nor snow, neither hail nor moisture, neither daybreak, nor highnoon nor night, no glory nor any radiance of day, but only the dazzling effulgence of the Highest in whose splendour all who are risen shall behold what shall be revealed unto them; for he hath ordained it to last for a septaine of years. Thus has it been determined, but alone to thee am I permitted to reveal what is to be.

Then did I answer and say, Yea, and I say now, O Lord, those who are still in life and able to keep what has been commanded by thee are alone to be esteemed happy. But what of them regarding whom my supplication was made, who among mankind is there that hath not done evil and broken thy commandments? for to me it appears that the life hereafter shall be fraught with bliss to but few, but with anguish to the greater number. For sin hath filled our hearts and hath seduced us from thee, leading us unto ruin and the eternal death, by those paths of the wicked which run far from the way of life, wherein are treading not only a few but almost all mankind of thy making.

Then did Uriel answer me and say, Lo, I will teach thee if thou wilt give attention to me, yea I will exhort thee even again and again, for the Highest

The Comparison of the Gems

hath not created one order of things but both [*the good and the evil*]. Seeing that thy lips hath said that the good are but few and the evildoers many, hearken to my words: if there be to thee as a possession one or two gems of rare price, wilt thou esteem as of greater value to them a larger number of stones that are of less value? To which I replied, O mighty one, what doth this mean? And he answered, For this question the earth and search of her diligently, and note what she revealeth unto thee. Say to her, Dost thou not yield gold and silver and copper, yea, iron and lead and potter's clay, and is not silver, being more common, less esteemed than gold, copper than silver, iron than copper, lead than iron, and potter's clay than lead? What then is to be esteemed the most, the things that are plentiful or those that are scarce?

Then did I reply, O Lord of Might, that is less precious which is more common, and of a truth what is scarce has the greater value. Then did he reply, Ponder on what thou hast said, for if he who hath that which is rarer vaunteth himself over him that possesseth what is more common, so also is the matter I have laid before thee for [the Highest saith] lo, I will rather glory over the few that by turning to me are saved (for in them shall my power be revealed), than sorrow over the multitude that go down to perdition, for they are even like the vapour of smoke, or a flame that consumeth, for

The Soul not created of the Dust

they appear but for a moment and then pass away for ever.

Then did I say, Earth, earth, why hast thou produced [us] if the soul of man is as the dust whereof all creatures are made? Better that the dust had been uncreated if the soul of man were made of naught but it! For the understanding soul expandeth within us, and through this we suffer anguish, because knowledge that we must pass away bringeth suffering. Therefore it is fitting that the beasts of the field should rejoice while mankind should sorrow, even all mankind should grieve while the animals are glad, inasmuch as a preferable lot is to them than to us, for they know not of the coming judgment nor of its result in anguish or bliss in the life to come. For what boots it for our life to be immortal if eternal anguish is its portion? All sons of men are corrupted with sin, and weighed down with transgressions. In such a case the wish is natural that there were no judgment to come.

Then did he [Uriel] reply and say, At the time that the Highest framed the earth and Adam and those descending from him, he ordained that there should be judgment of matters relating thereto. Now recall thine own saying, that the soul expandeth within us; for it is in consequence of this that the inhabitants of the world shall suffer anguish, inasmuch as they knowing good wrought evil, and recognising the statutes [of the Mightiest] did not observe them,

The Day of Judgment

ignoring the commands laid upon them. What plea will they advance in the day of judgment and what will be their reply at the last day? Hath not the Highest been for long time patient with the children of men, not so much for them but owing to the eternal decree which he had pre-ordained? Thereupon I did reply, Lo, O Lord, if I have found favour before thee, reveal this matter also unto me who am thy servant, either after death cometh, when having surrendered our soul we shall remain in sleep until those thy times shall arrive when all thy creation shall be re-created, or if it be thy will we shall suffer anguish at once.

Thereupon he [Uriel] made answer, Lo, even this too shall I unfold to thee, for thou art not one who associateth thyself with scoffers, nor dost ally thyself with those who shall suffer anguish. Though thou hast a balance of merit through good deeds remembered by the Highest, this shall not be declared unto thee until the last days of thy life, concerning which what thou must know is as follows—When the Highest has willed that a man's day of death has come, as the soul passeth from the body unto him who implanted it therein, then it worshippeth the Highest. If it be of those who have been contemners and breakers of the law of the Highest, throwing ridicule on his commandments and persecuting those that fear him, then such shall not obtain entrance into his mansions, but shall stray without in bitter

Sorrow of the Wicked: Joy of the Good

anguish, sorrowing with a *sorrow* sevenfold increased; first because they contemned the law of the Highest; second, because to them there can now be no return to the way of life; third, they behold the good things in store for those who have put faith in the promises of the Highest; fourth, because they see the sorrow in store for them at the end of things; fifth, because they behold the mansions of the blessed remaining in peace watched over by good angels; sixth, because they see some suffering anguish unspeakable even now; seventh and most terrible of all, because they are languishing in misery, overwhelmed with confusion of face and tormented with dread, inasmuch as they behold the glorious Almightiness of the Highest, whose law they transgressed while they were in the flesh, and before whom they must come for judgment at the end of things.

This is the condition of those who obeyed the will of the Highest, after the separation of soul and body. During the period of the flesh they diligently served the Highest, though at their peril each moment of time, and fully observed the statutes of him who is the Ruler. Accordingly this is the sentence regarding them: They shall behold with joy unspeakable the transcendent might of him who hath caught them up to be with himself, where their joy shall be sevenfold increased—first, because with constant watchfulness they have banished those vicious inclinations which tend to death, by mortifying the flesh

Joy of the Good whence they emanated; second, because they note the anxiety of the wicked over the penalty which awaiteth them; third, because they hear the testimony borne to their fidelity by him who created them; fourth, because they experience to the full the sweetness of that rest in the mansions [of the Highest] where, guarded by good angels, they await the reward promised them at the end of things; fifth, because their joy is complete to have been liberated from the bondage of corruptible flesh, to inherit the incorruptible glory to come; also because they behold the miseries of the earthly tabernacle from whose cramping restrictions they have been delivered, as compared with the liberty and joy of their free immortal state; sixth, it has been revealed to them that they shall shine as the face of the sun, that their glory shall be as that of the stars, shining as they will with a light that is undimmed; seventh and chiefly, because their joy shall be rooted in confidence that inasmuch as they were dauntless without presumption so they shall rejoice without dread, for they shall see the face of him whom it was their life-work to serve and from whom they trusted to obtain a sure recompence of bliss. The above, therefore, is the state of the spirits of the blessed, as well as the state of those who suffer anguish for evermore.

Then did I say unto him [Uriel], Shall there be an interval between the time when soul and body

Shall a Time of Pleading be given?

are separated and the revelation of the things regarding which thou hast spoken? Thereupon he [Uriel] made reply, Seven days shall be given wherein to see the matters of which thou hast been informed, and thereafter the souls of the departed shall be gathered unto their several places.

Then did I make answer, Lo, my Lord, if thy servant hath found grace before thee reveal unto him if in that day of judgment the blessed shall be permitted to plead for the transgressors unto the Highest —parents for children, children for parents, brothers for brothers, relatives for relatives, or men for those whom they love most dearly. To this Uriel replied, Since thou has found grace before me, lo, I shall reveal this also unto thee, that day of judgment is one when the uncertain shall be decided, when the truth shall be revealed regarding all flesh, for as no parent despatcheth his child, nor any son his parent, nor any lord his servant, nor any intimate friend him whom his soul loveth, that for him he may suffer illness, or sleep, or partake of food, or be cured of disease, so, in that day [of judgment] shall no one entreat for another, nor lay any burden of his sins on another, for all must bear their own lot, be it of righteousness or of transgression.

Then said I, Abraham prayed first for the Sodomites, and Moses for the fathers that sinned in the wilderness: and Jesus after him for Israel in the time of Achan: and Samuel and David for the

The Present Life not the End of the Soul

destruction: and Solomon for them that should come to the sanctuary: and Helias for those that received rain; and for the dead, that he might live: and Ezechias for the people in the time of Sennacherib: and many for many. Even so now, seeing corruption is grown up, and wickedness increased, and the righteous have prayed for the ungodly: wherefore shall it not be so now also?

He answered me, and said, This present life is not the end where much glory doth abide; therefore have they prayed for the weak. But the day of doom shall be the end of this time, and the beginning of the immortality for to come, wherein corruption is past, intemperance is at an end, infidelity is cut off, righteousness is grown, and truth is sprung up. Then shall no man be able to save him that is destroyed, nor to oppress him that hath gotten the victory.

I answered then and said, This is my first and last saying, that it had been better not to have given the earth unto Adam: or else, when it was given him, to have restrained him from sinning. For what profit is it for men now in this present time to live in heaviness, and after death to look for punishment? O thou Adam, what hast thou done? for though it was thou that sinned, thou art not fallen alone, but we all that come of thee. For what profit is it unto us, if there be promised us an immortal time, whereas we have done the works that bring death? And that there is promised us an everlasting hope,

The Joys of Paradise

whereas ourselves being most wicked are made vain? And that there are laid up for us dwellings of health and safety, whereas we have lived wickedly? And that the glory of the Most High is kept to defend them which have led a wary life, whereas we have walked in the most wicked ways of all? And that there should be shewed a paradise, whose fruit endureth for ever, wherein is security and medicine, since we shall not enter into it? (for we have walked in unpleasant places.) And that the faces of them which have used abstinence shall shine above the stars, whereas our faces shall be blacker than darkness? For while we lived and committed iniquity, we considered not that we should begin to suffer for it after death.

Then answered he me, and said, This is the condition of the battle, which man that is born upon the earth shall fight; that, if he be overcome, he shall suffer as thou hast said: but if he get the victory, he shall receive the thing that I say. For this is the life whereof Moses spake unto the people while he lived, saying, Choose thee life, that thou mayest live. Nevertheless they believed not him, nor yet the prophets after him, no nor me which have spoken unto them, that there should not be such heaviness in their destruction, as shall be joy over them that are persuaded to salvation.

I answered then, and said, I know, Lord, that the Most High is called merciful, in that he hath mercy

This World is for the Many, the Next for the Few

upon them which are not yet come into the world, and upon those also that turn to his law; and that he is patient, and long suffereth those that have sinned, as his creatures; and that he is bountiful, for he is ready to give where it needeth; and that he is of great mercy, for he multiplieth more and more mercies to them that are present, and that are past, and also to them which are to come. For if he shall not multiply his mercies, the world would not continue with them that inherit therein. And he pardoneth; for if he did not so of his goodness, that they which have committed iniquities might be eased of them, the ten thousandth part of men should not remain living. And being judge, if he should not forgive them that are cured with his word, and put out the multitude of contentions, there should be very few left peradventure in an innumerable multitude.

* And he answered me, saying, The Most High hath made this world for many, but the world to come for few. I will tell thee a similitude, Esdras; As when thou askest the earth, it shall say unto thee, that it giveth much mould whereof earthen vessels are made, but little dust that gold cometh of: even so is the course of this present world. There be many created, but few shall be saved.

So answered I and said, Swallow then down, O my soul, understanding, and devour wisdom. For thou hast agreed to give ear, and art willing to prophesy: for thou hast no longer space than only to

We are His Workmanship

live. O Lord, if thou suffer not thy servant, that we may pray before thee, and thou give us seed unto our heart, and culture to our understanding, that there may come fruit of it; how shall each man live that is corrupt, who beareth the place of a man? For thou art alone, and we all one workmanship of thine hands, like as thou hast said. For when the body is fashioned now in the mother's womb, and thou givest it members, thy creature is preserved in fire and water, and nine months doth thy workmanship endure thy creature which is created in her. But that which keepeth and is kept shall both be preserved: and when the time cometh, the womb preserved delivereth up the things that grew in it. For thou hast commanded out of the parts of the body, that is to say, out of the breasts, milk to be given, which is the fruit of the breasts, that the thing which is fashioned may be nourished for a time, till thou disposest it to thy mercy. Thou broughtest it up with thy righteousness, and nurturedst it in thy law, and reformedst it with thy judgment. And thou shalt mortify it as thy creature, and quicken it as thy work. If therefore thou shalt destroy him which with so great labour was fashioned, it is an easy thing to be ordained by thy commandment, that the thing which was made might be preserved. Now therefore, Lord, I will speak; touching man in general, thou knowest best; but touching thy people, for whose sake I am sorry; and for thine inheritance, for whose cause I mourn; and for Israel, for whom

God's Eternal Purpose

I am heavy; and for Jacob, for whose sake I am troubled; therefore will I begin to pray before thee for myself and for them: for I see the falls of us that dwell in the land. But I have heard the swiftness of the judge which is to come. Therefore hear my voice, and understand my words, and I shall speak before thee.

This is the beginning of the words of Esdras, before he was taken up: and I said,

O Lord, thou that dwellest in everlastingness, which beholdest from above things in the heaven and in the air; whose throne is inestimable; whose glory may not be comprehended; before whom the hosts of angels stand with trembling, whose service is conversant in wind and fire; whose word is true, and sayings constant; whose commandment is strong, and ordinance fearful; whose look drieth up the depths, and indignation maketh the mountains to melt away; which the truth witnesseth: O hear the prayer of thy servant, and give ear to the petition of thy creature. For while I live I will speak, and so long as I have understanding I will answer. O look not upon the sins of thy people; but on them which serve thee in truth. Regard not the wicked inventions of the heathen, but the desire of those that keep thy testimonies in afflictions. Think not upon those that have walked feignedly before thee: but remember them, which according to thy will have known thy fear. Let it not be thy will to destroy them which

Goodness & Mercy well-pleasing to God

have lived like beasts; but to look upon them that have clearly taught thy law. Take thou no indignation at them which are deemed worse than beasts; but love them that alway put their trust in thy righteousness and glory. For we and our fathers do languish of such diseases: but because of us sinners thou shalt be called merciful. For if thou hast a desire to have mercy upon us, thou shalt be called merciful, to us namely, that have no works of righteousness. For the just, which have many good works laid up with thee, shall out of their own deeds receive reward. For what is man, that thou shouldest take displeasure at him? or what is a corruptible generation, that thou shouldest be so bitter toward it? For in truth there is no man among them that be born, but he hath dealt wickedly; and among the faithful there is none which hath not done amiss. For in this, O Lord, thy righteousness and thy goodness shall be declared, if thou be merciful unto them which have not the confidence of good works.

Then answered he me, and said, Some things hast thou spoken aright, and according unto thy words it shall be. For indeed I will not think on the disposition of them which have sinned before death, before judgment, before destruction: but I will rejoice over the disposition of the righteous, and I will remember also their pilgrimage, and the salvation, and the reward, that they shall have. Like as I have spoken now, so shall it come to pass. For as

Esdras entreats Mercy for God's Creatures

the husbandman soweth much seed upon the ground, and planteth many trees, and yet the thing that is sown good in his season cometh not up, neither doth all that is planted take root: even so is it of them that are sown in the world; they shall not all be saved.

I answered then and said, If I have found grace, let me speak. Like as the husbandman's seed perisheth, if it come not up, and receive not thy rain in due season; or if there come too much rain, and corrupt it: even so perisheth man also, which is formed with thy hands, and is called thine own image, because thou art like unto him, for whose sake thou hast made all things, and likened him unto the husbandman's seed. Be not wroth with us, but spare thy people, and have mercy upon thine own inheritance: for thou art merciful unto thy creature.

Then answered he me, and said, Things present are for the present, and things to come for such as be to come. For thou comest far short that thou shouldest be able to love my creature more than I: but I have ofttimes drawn nigh unto thee, and unto it, but never to the unrighteous. In this also thou art marvellous before the Most High: in that thou hast humbled thyself, as it becometh thee, and hast not judged thyself worthy to be much glorified among the righteous. For many great miseries shall be done to them that in the latter time shall dwell in the world, because they have walked in great pride.

Uriel warneth Esdras not to ask too much

But understand thou for thyself, and seek out the glory for such as be like thee. For unto you is paradise opened, the tree of life is planted, the time to come is prepared, plenteousness is made ready, a city is builded, and rest is allowed, yea, perfect goodness and wisdom. The root of evil is sealed up from you, weakness and the moth is hid from you, and corruption is fled into hell to be forgotten: sorrows are passed, and in the end is shewed the treasure of immortality. And therefore ask thou no more questions concerning the multitude of them that perish. For when they had taken liberty, they despised the Most High, thought scorn of his law, and forsook his ways. Moreover they have trodden down his righteous, and said in their heart, that there is no God; yea, and that knowing they must die. For as the things aforesaid shall receive you, so thirst and pain are prepared for them: for it was not his will that men should come to nought: but they which be created have defiled the name of him that made them, and were unthankful unto him which prepared life for them. And therefore is my judgment now at hand. These things have I not shewed unto all men, but unto thee, and a few like thee.

Then answered I and said, Behold, O Lord, now hast thou shewed me the multitude of the wonders, which thou wilt begin to do in the last times: but at what time, thou hast not shewed me.

Uriel describes the Day of the Lord*

He answered me then, and said, Measure thou the time diligently in itself: and when thou seest part of the signs past, which I have told thee before, then shalt thou understand, that it is the very same time, wherein the Highest will begin to visit the world which he made. Therefore when there shall be seen earthquakes and uproars of the people in the world: then shalt thou well understand, that the Most High spake of those things from the days that were before thee, even from the beginning. For like as all that is made in the world hath a beginning and an end, and the end is manifest: even so the times also of the Highest have plain beginnings in wonders and powerful works, and endings in effects and signs. And every one that shall be saved, and shall be able to escape by his works, and by faith, whereby ye have believed, shall be preserved from the said perils, and shall see my salvation in my land, and within my borders: for I have sanctified them for me from the beginning. Then shall they be in pitiful case, which now have abused my ways: and they that have cast them away despitefully shall dwell in torments. For such as in their life have received benefits, and have not known me; and they that have lothed my law, while they had yet liberty, and, when as yet place of repentance was open unto them, understood not, but despised it; the same must know it after death by pain. And therefore be thou not curious how the ungodly shall be

Man's Devices bring Death

punished, and when: but enquire how the righteous shall be saved, whose the world is, and for whom the world is created.

Then answered I and said, I have said before, and now do speak, and will speak it also hereafter, that there be many more of them which perish, than of them which shall be saved: like as a wave is greater than a drop.

And he answered me, saying, Like as the field is, so is also the seed; as the flowers be, such are the colours also; such as the workman is, such also is the work; and as the husbandman is himself, so is his husbandry also: for it was the time of the world. And now when I prepared the world, which was not yet made, even for them to dwell in that now live, no man spake against me. For then every one obeyed: but now the manners of them which are created in this world that is made are corrupted by a perpetual seed, and by a law which is unsearchable rid themselves. So I considered the world, and, behold, there was peril because of the devices that were come into it. And I saw, and spared it greatly, and have kept me a grape of the cluster, and a plant of a great people. Let the multitude perish then, which was born in vain; and let my grape be kept, and my plant; for with great labour have I made it perfect. Nevertheless, if thou wilt cease yet seven days more, (but thou shalt not fast in them, but go into a field of flowers, where no house is

Esdras goeth unto Ardath

builded, and eat only the flowers of the field; taste no flesh, drink no wine, but eat flowers only;) and pray unto the highest continually, then will I come and talk with thee.

So I went my way into the field which is called Ardath, like as he commanded me; and there I sat among the flowers, and did eat of the herbs of the field, and the meat of the same satisfied me. After seven days I sat upon the grass, and my heart was vexed within me, like as before: and I opened my mouth, and began to talk before the Most High, and said,

O Lord, thou that shewest thyself unto us, thou wast shewed unto our fathers in the wilderness, in a place where no man treadeth, in a barren place, when they came out of Egypt. And thou spakest, saying, Hear me, O Israel; and mark my words, thou seed of Jacob. For, behold, I sow my law in you, and it shall bring fruit in you, and ye shall be honoured in it for ever. But our fathers, which received the law, kept it not, and observed not thy ordinances: and though the fruit of thy law did not perish, neither could it, for it was thine; yet they that received it perished, because they kept not the thing that was sown in them. And, lo, it is a custom, when the ground hath received seed, or the sea a ship, or any vessel meat or drink, that, that being perished wherein it was sown or cast into, that thing also which was sown, or cast therein, or

What Esdras saw in Ardath

received, doth perish, and remaineth not with us: but with us it hath not happened so. For we that have received the law perish by sin, and our heart also which received it. Notwithstanding the law perisheth not, but remaineth in his force.

And when I spake these things in my heart, I looked back with mine eyes, and upon the right side I saw a woman, and, behold, she mourned and wept with a loud voice, and was much grieved in heart, and her clothes were rent, and she had ashes upon her head. Then let I my thoughts go that I was in, and turned me unto her, and said unto her, Wherefore weepest thou? Why art thou so grieved in thy mind?

And she said unto me, Sir, let me alone, that I may bewail myself, and add unto my sorrow, for I am sore vexed in my mind, and brought very low.

And I said unto her, What aileth thee? tell me.

She said unto me, I thy servant have been barren, and had no child, though I had an husband thirty years. And those thirty years I did nothing else day and night, and every hour, but make my prayer to the Highest. After thirty years God heard me thine handmaid, looked upon my misery, considered my trouble, and gave me a son: and I was very glad of him, so was my husband also, and all my neighbours: and we gave great honour unto the Almighty. And I nourished him with great travail. So when he grew up, and came to the time that he should

The Sorrow of he Woman of Ardath

have a wife, I made a feast. * And it so came to pass, that when my son was entered into his wedding chamber, he fell down, and died. Then we all overthrew the lights, and all my neighbours rose up to comfort me: so I took my rest unto the second day at night. And it came to pass, when they had all left off to comfort me, to the end I might be quiet; then rose I up by night, and fled, and came hither into this field, as thou seest. And I do now purpose not to return into the city, but here to stay, and neither to eat nor drink, but continually to mourn and to fast until I die.

Then left I the meditations wherein I was, and spake to her in anger, saying, Thou foolish woman above all other, seest thou not our mourning, and what happeneth unto us? How that Sion our mother is full of all heaviness, and much humbled, mourning very sore? And now, seeing we all mourn and are sad, for we are all in heaviness, art thou grieved for one son? For ask the earth, and she shall tell thee, that it is she which ought to mourn for the fall of so many that grow upon her. For out of her came all at the first, and out of her shall all others come, and, behold, they walk almost all into destruction, and a multitude of them is utterly rooted out. Who then should make more mourning than she, that hath lost so great a multitude; and not thou, which art sorry but for one? But if thou sayest unto me, My lamentation is not like the

Esdras exhorteth the Woman

earth's, because I have lost the fruit of my womb, which I brought forth with pains, and bare with sorrows; but the earth *not so:* for the multitude present in it according to the course of the earth is gone, as it came: then say I unto thee, Like as thou hast brought forth with labour; even so the earth also hath given her fruit, namely, man, ever since the beginning unto him that made her. Now therefore keep thy sorrow to thyself, and bear with a good courage that which hath befallen thee. For if thou shalt acknowledge the determination of God to be just, thou shalt both receive thy son in time, and shalt be commended among women. Go thy way then into the city to thine husband.

And she said unto me, That will I not do: I will not go into the city, but here will I die.

So I proceeded to speak further unto her, and said, Do not so, but be counselled by me: for how many are the adversities of Sion? be comforted in regard of the sorrow of Jerusalem. For thou seest that our sanctuary is laid waste, our altar broken down, our temple destroyed; our psaltery is laid on the ground, our song is put to silence, our rejoicing is at an end, the light of our candlestick is put out, the ark of our covenant is spoiled, our holy things are defiled, and the name that is called upon us is almost profaned: our children are put to shame, our priests are burnt, our Levites are gone into captivity, our virgins are defiled, and our wives ravished; our

Where is Uriel the Angel?

righteous men carried away, our little ones destroyed, our young men are brought in bondage, and our strong men are become weak; and, which is the greatest of all, the seal of Sion hath now lost her honour; for she is delivered into the hands of them that hate us. And therefore shake off thy great heaviness, and put away the multitude of sorrows, that the Mighty may be merciful unto thee again, and the Highest shall give thee rest and ease from thy labour.

And it came to pass, while I was talking with her, behold, her face upon a sudden shined exceedingly, and her countenance glistened, so that I was afraid of her, and mused what it might be. And, behold, suddenly she made a great cry very fearful: so that the earth shook at the noise of the woman. And I looked, and, behold, the woman appeared unto me no more, but there was a city builded, and a large place shewed itself from the foundations: then was I afraid, and cried with a loud voice, and said, Where is Uriel the angel, who came unto me at the first? for he hath caused me to fall into many trances, and mine end is turned into corruption, and my prayer to rebuke.

And as I was speaking these words, behold, he came unto me, and looked upon me. And, lo, I lay as one that had been dead, and mine understanding was taken from me: and he took me by the right hand, and comforted me, and set me upon my

The Lor praises Esdras unfolds th Vision

feet, and said unto me, What aileth thee? and why art thou so disquieted? and why is thine understanding troubled, and the thoughts of thine heart?

And I said, Because thou hast forsaken me, and yet I did according to thy words, and I went into the field, and, lo, I have seen, and yet see, that I am not able to express.

And he said unto me, Stand up manfully, and I will advise thee.

Then said I, Speak on, my lord, in me; only forsake me not, lest I die frustrate of my hope. For I have seen that I knew not, and hear that I do not know. Or is my sense deceived, or my soul in a dream? Now therefore I beseech thee that thou wilt shew thy servant of this vision.

He answered me then, and said, Hear me, and I shall inform thee, and tell thee wherefore thou art afraid: for the Highest will reveal many secret things unto thee. He hath seen that thy way is right: for that thou sorrowest continually for thy people, and makest great lamentation for Sion. This therefore is the meaning of the vision which thou lately sawest: Thou sawest a woman mourning, and thou begannest to comfort her: but now seest thou the likeness of the woman no more, but there appeared unto thee a city builded. And whereas she told thee of the death of her son, this is the solution: This woman, whom thou sawest, is Sion: and whereas she said unto thee, even she whom thou seest as a

Meaning of the Vision of the Woman

city builded, whereas, *I say,* she said unto thee, that she hath been thirty years barren: those are the thirty years wherein there was no offering made in her. But after thirty years Solomon builded the city, and offered offerings: and then bare the barren a son. And whereas she told thee that she nourished him with labour: that was the dwelling in Jerusalem. But whereas she said unto thee, That my son coming into his marriage chamber happened to have a fall, and died: this was the destruction that came to Jerusalem. And, behold, thou sawest her likeness, and because she mourned for her son, thou begannest to comfort her: and of these things which have chanced, these are to be opened unto thee. For now the Most High seeth that thou art grieved unfeignedly, and sufferest from thy whole heart for her, so hath he shewed thee the brightness of her glory, and the comeliness of her beauty: and therefore I bade thee remain in the field where no house was builded: for I knew that the Highest would shew this unto thee. Therefore I commanded thee to go into the field, where no foundation of any building was. For in the place wherein the Highest beginneth to shew his city, there can no man's building be able to stand. And therefore fear not, let not thine heart be affrighted, but go thy way in, and see the beauty and greatness of the building, as much as thine eyes be able to see: and then shalt thou hear as much as thine ears may comprehend.

The Vision of the Eagle

For thou art blessed above many other, and art called with the Highest; and so are but few. But to morrow at night thou shalt remain here; and so shall the Highest shew thee visions of the high things, which the Most High will do unto them that dwell upon earth in the last days.

So I slept that night and another, like as he commanded me. * Then saw I a dream, and, behold, there came up from the sea an eagle, which had twelve feathered wings, and three heads. And I saw, and, behold, she spread her wings over all the earth, and all the winds of the air blew on her, and were gathered together. And I beheld, and out of her feathers there grew other contrary feathers; and they became little feathers and small. But her heads were at rest: the head in the midst was greater than the other, yet rested it with the residue. Moreover I beheld, and, lo, the eagle flew with her feathers, and reigned upon earth, and over them that dwelt therein. And I saw that all things under heaven were subject unto her, and no man spake against her, no, not one creature upon earth. And I beheld, and, lo, the eagle rose upon her talons, and spake to her feathers, saying,

Watch not all at once: sleep every one in his own place, and watch by course: but let the heads be preserved for the last. And I beheld, and, lo, the voice went not out of her heads, but from the midst of her body. And I numbered her contrary feathers,

The Vision of the Eagle

and, behold, there were eight of them. And I looked, and, behold, on the right side there arose one feather, and reigned over all the earth; and so it was, that when it reigned, the end of it came, and the place thereof appeared no more: so the next following stood up, and reigned, and had a great time; and it happened, that when it reigned, the end of it came also, like as the first, so that it appeared no more.

Then came there a voice unto it, and said, Hear thou that hast borne rule over the earth so long: this I say unto thee, before thou beginnest to appear no more, there shall none after thee attain unto thy time, neither unto the half thereof. Then arose the third, and reigned as the other before, and appeared no more also. So went it with all the residue one after another, as that every one reigned, and then appeared no more.

Then I beheld, and, lo, in process of time the feathers that followed stood up upon the right side, that they might rule also; and some of them ruled, but within a while they appeared no more: for some of them were set up, but ruled not. After this I looked, and, behold, the twelve feathers appeared no more, nor the two little feathers: and there was no more upon the eagle's body, but three heads that rested, and six little wings. Then saw I also that two little feathers divided themselves from the six, and remained under the head that was upon the right

The Vision of the Eagle

side: for the four continued in their place. And I beheld, and, lo, the feathers that were under the wing thought to set up themselves, and to have the rule. And I beheld, and, lo, there was one set up, but shortly it appeared no more. And the second was sooner away than the first. And I beheld, and, lo, the two that remained thought also in themselves to reign:

And when they so thought, behold, there awaked one of the heads that were at rest, namely, it that was in the midst; for that was greater than the two other heads. And then I saw that the two other heads were joined with it. And, behold, the head was turned with them that were with it, and did eat up the two feathers under the wing that would have reigned. But this head put the whole earth in fear, and bare rule in it over all those that dwelt upon the earth with much oppression; and it had the governance of the world more than all the wings that had been. And after this I beheld, and, lo, the head that was in the midst suddenly appeared no more, like as the wings. But there remained the two heads, which also in like sort ruled upon the earth, and over those that dwelt therein. And I beheld, and, lo, the head upon the right side devoured it that was upon the left side.

Then I heard a voice, which said unto me, Look before thee, and consider the thing that thou seest. And I beheld, and lo as it were a roaring lion

The Lion and the Eagle

chased out of the wood: and I saw that he sent out a man's voice unto the eagle, and said, Hear thou, I will talk with thee, and the Highest shall say unto thee, Art not thou it that remainest of the four beasts, whom I made to reign in my world, that the end of their times might come through them? And the fourth came, and overcame all the beasts that were past, and had power over the world with great fearfulness, and over the whole compass of the earth with much wicked oppression; and so long time dwelt he upon the earth with deceit. For the earth hast thou not judged with truth. For thou hast afflicted the meek, thou hast hurt the peaceable, thou hast loved liars, and destroyed the dwellings of them that brought forth fruit, and hast cast down the walls of such as did thee no harm. Therefore is thy wrongful dealing come up unto the Highest, and thy pride unto the Mighty. The Highest also hath looked upon the proud times, and, behold, they are ended, and his abominations are fulfilled. And therefore appear no more, thou eagle, nor thy horrible wings, nor thy wicked feathers, nor thy malicious heads, nor thy hurtful claws, nor all thy vain body: that all the earth may be refreshed, and may return, being delivered from thy violence, and that she may hope for the judgment and mercy of him that made her.

* And it came to pass, whiles the lion spake these words unto the eagle, I saw, and, behold, the head

Interpretation of the Vision

that remained and the four wings appeared no more, and the two went unto it, and set themselves up to reign, and their kingdom was small, and full of uproar. And I saw, and, behold, they appeared no more, and the whole body of the eagle was burnt, so that the earth was in great fear: then awaked I out of the trouble and trance of my mind, and from great fear, and said unto my spirit, Lo, this hast thou done unto me, in that thou searchest out the ways of the Highest. Lo, yet am I weary in my mind, and very weak in my spirit; and little strength is there in me, for the great fear wherewith I was affrighted this night. Therefore will I now beseech the Highest, that he will comfort me unto the end.

And I said, Lord that bearest rule, if I have found grace before thy sight, and if I am justified with thee before many others, and if my prayer indeed be come up before thy face; comfort me then, and shew me thy servant the interpretation and plain difference of this fearful vision, that thou mayest perfectly comfort my soul. For thou hast judged me worthy to shew me the last times.

And he said unto me, This is the interpretation of the vision: The eagle, whom thou sawest come up from the sea, is the kingdom which was seen in the vision of thy brother Daniel. But it was not expounded unto him, therefore now I declare it unto thee. Behold, the days will come, that there shall rise up a kingdom upon earth, and it shall be feared

Interpretation of the Vision

above all the kingdoms that were before it. In the same shall twelve kings reign, one after another: whereof the second shall begin to reign, and shall have more time than any of the twelve. And this do the twelve wings signify, which thou sawest. As for the voice which thou heardest speak, and that thou sawest not to go out from the heads, but from the midst of the body thereof, this is the interpretation: That after the time of that kingdom there shall arise great strivings, and it shall stand in peril of falling: nevertheless it shall not then fall, but shall be restored again to his beginning. And whereas thou sawest the eight small under feathers sticking to her wings, this is the interpretation: That in him there shall arise eight kings, whose times shall be but small, and their years swift. And two of them shall perish, the middle time approaching: four shall be kept until their end begin to approach: but two shall be kept unto the end. And whereas thou sawest three heads resting, this is the interpretation: In his last days shall the Most High raise up three kingdoms, and renew many things therein, and they shall have the dominion of the earth, and of those that dwell therein, with much oppression, above all those that were before them: therefore are they called the heads of the eagle. For these are they that shall accomplish his wickedness, and that shall finish his last end.

And whereas thou sawest that the great head

Interpretation of the Vision

appeared no more, it signifieth that one of them shall die upon his bed, and yet with pain. For the two that remain shall be slain with the sword. For the sword of the one shall devour the other: but at the last shall he fall through the sword himself.

And whereas thou sawest two feathers under the wings passing over the head that is on the right side; it signifieth that these are they, whom the Highest hath kept unto their end: this is the small kingdom and full of trouble, as thou sawest. And the lion, whom thou sawest rising up out of the wood, and roaring, and speaking to the eagle, and rebuking her for her unrighteousness with all the words which thou has heard; this is the anointed, which the Highest hath kept for them and for their wickedness unto the end: he shall reprove them, and shall upbraid them with their cruelty. For he shall set them before him alive in judgment, and shall rebuke them, and correct them. For the rest of my people shall he deliver with mercy, those that have been preserved upon my borders, and he shall make them joyful until the coming of the day of judgment, whereof I have spoken unto thee from the beginning.

This is the dream that thou sawest, and these are the interpretations. Thou only hast been meet to know this secret of the Highest. Therefore write all these things that thou hast seen in a book, and hide them: and teach them to the wise of the people, whose hearts thou knowest may comprehend and

The People go to Esdras for Comfort

keep these secrets. But wait thou here thyself yet seven days more, that it may be shewed thee, whatsoever it pleaseth the Highest to declare unto thee. And with that he went his way.

And it came to pass, when all the people saw that the seven days were past, and I not come again into the city, they gathered them all together, from the least unto the greatest, and came unto me, and said, What have we offended thee? and what evil have we done against thee, that thou forsakest us, and sittest here in this place? For of all the prophets thou only art left us, as a cluster of the vintage, and as a candle in a dark place, and as a haven or ship preserved from the tempest. Are not the evils which are come to us sufficient? If thou shalt forsake us, how much better had it been for us, if we also had been burned in the midst of Sion? For we are not better than they that died there. And they wept with a loud voice.

Then answered I them, and said, Be of good comfort, O Israel; and be not heavy, thou house of Jacob: for the Highest hath you in remembrance, and the Mighty hath not forgotten you in temptation. As for me, I have not forsaken you, neither am I departed from you: but am come into this place, to pray for the desolation of Sion, and that I might seek mercy for the low estate of your sanctuary. And now go your way home every man, and after these days will I come unto you.

The Vision of the Man of the Sea

So the people went their way into the city, like as I commanded them: but I remained still in the field seven days, as the angel commanded me; and did eat only in those days of the flowers of the field, and had my meat of the herbs.

* And it came to pass after seven days, I dreamed a dream by night: and, lo, there arose a wind from the sea, that it moved all the waves thereof. And I beheld, and, lo, that man waxed strong with the thousands of heaven: and when he turned his countenance to look, all the things trembled that were seen under him. And whensoever the voice went out of his mouth, all they burned that heard his voice, like as the earth faileth when it feeleth the fire.

And after this I beheld, and, lo, there was gathered together a multitude of men, out of number, from the four winds of the heaven, to subdue the man that came out of the sea. But I beheld, and, lo, he had graved himself a great mountain, and flew up upon it. But I would have seen the region or place whereout the hill was graven, and I could not.

And after this I beheld, and, lo, all they which were gathered together to subdue him were sore afraid, and yet durst fight. And, lo, as he saw the violence of the multitude that came, he neither lifted up his hand, nor held sword, nor any instrument of war: but only I saw that he sent out of his mouth

Esdras awakes out of the Vision

as it had been a blast of fire, and out of his lips a flaming breath, and out of his tongue he cast out sparks and tempests. And they were all mixed together; the blast of fire, the flaming breath and the great tempest; and fell with violence upon the multitude which was prepared to fight, and burned them up every one, so that upon a sudden of an innumerable multitude nothing was to be perceived, but only dust and smell of smoke: when I saw this I was afraid.

Afterward saw I the same man come down from the mountain, and call unto him another peaceable multitude. And there came much people unto him, whereof some were glad, some were sorry, some of them were bound, and other some brought of them that were offered: then was I sick through great fear, and I awaked, and said,

Thou hast shewed thy servant these wonders from the beginning, and hast counted me worthy that thou shouldest receive my prayer: shew me now yet the interpretation of this dream. For as I conceive in mine understanding, woe unto them that shall be left in those days! and much more woe unto them that are not left behind! For they that were not left were in heaviness. Now understand I the things that are laid up in the latter days, which shall happen unto them, and to those that are left behind. Therefore are they come into great perils and many necessities, like as these dreams declare. Yet is it

Interpretation of the Vision

easier for him that is in danger to come into these things, than to pass away as a cloud out of the world, and not to see the things that happen in the last days.

And he answered unto me, and said, The interpretation of the vision shall I shew thee, and I will open unto thee the thing that thou hast required. Whereas thou hast spoken of them that are left behind, this is the interpretation: He that shall endure the peril in that time hath kept himself: they that be fallen into danger are such as have works, and faith toward the Almighty. Know this therefore, that they which be left behind are more blessed than they that be dead. This is the meaning of the vision: Whereas thou sawest a man coming up from the midst of the sea: the same is he whom God the Highest hath kept a great season, which by his own self shall deliver his creature: and he shall order them that are left behind. And whereas thou sawest, that out of his mouth there came as a blast of wind, and fire, and storm; and that he held neither sword, nor any instrument of war, but that the rushing in of him destroyed the whole multitude that came to subdue him; this is the interpretation: Behold, the days come, when the Most High will begin to deliver them that are upon the earth. And he shall come to the astonishment of them that dwell on the earth. And one shall undertake to fight against another, one city against another, one place

Interpretation of the Vision

against another, one people against another, and one realm against another. And the time shall be when these things shall come to pass, and the signs shall happen which I shewed thee before, and then shall my Son be declared, whom thou sawest as a man ascending. And when all the people hear his voice, every man shall in their own land leave the battle they have one against another. And an innumerable multitude shall be gathered together, as thou sawest them, willing to come, and to overcome him by fighting. But he shall stand upon the top of the mount Sion. And Sion shall come, and shall be shewed to all men, being prepared and builded, like as thou sawest the hill graven without hands. And this my Son shall rebuke the wicked inventions of those nations, which for their wicked life are fallen into the tempest; and shall lay before them their evil thoughts, and the torments wherewith they shall begin to be tormented, which are like unto a flame: and he shall destroy them without labour by the law which is like unto fire.

And whereas thou sawest that he gathered another peaceable multitude unto him; those are the ten tribes, which were carried away prisoners out of their own land in the time of Osea the king, whom Salmanasar the king of Assyria led away captive, and he carried them over the waters, and so came they into another land. But they took this counsel among themselves, that they would leave the multi-

No Man can see the Son of God

tude of the heathen, and go forth into a further country, where never mankind dwelt, that they might there keep their statutes, which they never kept in their own land. And they entered into Euphrates by the narrow passages of the river. For the Most High then shewed signs for them, and held still the flood, till they were passed over. For through that country there was a great way to go, namely, of a year and a half: and the same region is called Arsareth. Then dwelt they there until the latter time; and now when they shall begin to come, the Highest shall stay the springs of the stream again, that they may go through: therefore sawest thou the multitude with peace. But those that be left behind of thy people are they that are found within my borders. Now when he destroyeth the multitude of the nations that are gathered together, he shall defend his people that remain. And then shall he shew them great wonders.

Then said I, O Lord that bearest rule, shew me this: Wherefore have I seen the man coming up from the midst of the sea?

And he said unto me, Like as thou canst neither seek out nor know the things that are in the deep of the sea: even so can no man upon earth see my Son, or those that be with him, but in the day time. This is the interpretation of the dream which thou sawest, and whereby thou only art here lightened. For thou hast forsaken thine own way, and applied

God speaks to Esdras

thy diligence unto my law, and sought it. Thy life hast thou ordered in wisdom, and hast called understanding thy mother. And therefore have I shewed thee the treasures of the Highest: after other three days I will speak other things unto thee, and declare unto thee mighty and wondrous things.

Then went I forth into the field, giving praise and thanks greatly unto the Most High because of his wonders, which he did in time; and because he governeth the same, and such things as fall in their seasons: and there I sat three days.

* And it came to pass upon the third day, I sat under an oak, and, behold, there came a voice out of a bush over against me, and said, Esdras, Esdras. And I said, Here am I, Lord. And I stood up upon my feet.

Then said he unto me, In the bush I did manifestly reveal myself unto Moses, and talked with him, when my people served in Egypt: and I sent him, and led my people out of Egypt, and brought him up to the mount of Sinai, where I held him by me a long season, and told him many wondrous things, and shewed him the secrets of the times, and the end; and commanded him, saying, These words shalt thou declare, and these shalt thou hide. And now I say unto thee, That thou lay up in thy heart the signs that I have shewed, and the dreams that thou hast seen, and the interpretations which thou hast heard: for thou shalt be taken away from all, and from

Prophecy of Evils to come

henceforth thou shalt remain with my Son, and with such as be like thee, until the times be ended. For the world hath lost his youth, and the times begin to wax old. For the world is divided into twelve parts, and the ten parts of it are gone already, and half of a tenth part: and there remaineth that which is after the half of the tenth part. Now therefore set thine house in order, and reprove thy people, comfort such of them as be in trouble, and now renounce corruption, let go from thee mortal thoughts, cast away the burdens of man, put off now the weak nature, and set aside the thoughts that are most heavy unto thee, and haste thee to flee from these times. For yet greater evils than those which thou hast seen happen shall be done hereafter. For look how much the world shall be weaker through age, so much the more shall evils increase upon them that dwell therein. For the truth is fled far away, and leasing is hard at hand: for now hasteth the vision to come, which thou hast seen.

Then answered I before thee, and said, Behold, Lord, I will go, as thou hast commanded me, and reprove the people which are present: but they that shall be born afterward, who shall admonish them? thus the world is set in darkness, and they that dwell therein are without light. For thy law is burnt, therefore no man knoweth the things that are done of thee, or the works that shall begin. But if I have found grace before thee, send the Holy Ghost

The Task of Esdras

into me, and I shall write all that hath been done in the world since the beginning, which were written in thy law, that men may find thy path, and that they which will live in the latter days may live.

And he answered me, saying, Go thy way, gather the people together, and say unto them, that they seek thee not for forty days. But look thou prepare thee many box trees, and take with thee Sarea, Dabria, Selemia, Ecanus, and Asiel, these five which are ready to write swiftly; and come hither, and I shall light a candle of understanding in thine heart, which shall not be put out, till the things be performed which thou shalt begin to write. And when thou hast done, some things shalt thou publish, and some things shalt thou shew secretly to the wise: to morrow this hour shalt thou begin to write.

Then went I forth, as he commanded, and gathered all the people together, and said, Hear these words, O Israel. Our fathers at the beginning were strangers in Egypt, from whence they were delivered: and received the law of life, which they kept not, which ye also have transgressed after them. Then was the land, even the land of Sion, parted among you by lot: but your fathers, and ye yourselves, have done unrighteousness, and have not kept the ways which the Highest commanded you. And forasmuch as he is a righteous judge, he took from you in time the thing that he had given you. And now are ye here, and your brethren among

The Cup of Understanding

you. Therefore if so be that ye will subdue your own understanding, and reform your hearts, ye shall be kept alive, and after death ye shall obtain mercy. For after death shall the judgment come, when we shall live again: and then shall the names of the righteous be manifest, and the works of the ungodly shall be declared. Let no man therefore come unto me now, nor seek after me these forty days.

So I took the five men, as he commanded me, and we went into the field, and remained there. And the next day, behold, a voice called me, saying, Esdras, open thy mouth, and drink that I give thee to drink. Then opened I my mouth, and, behold, he reached me a full cup, which was full as it were with water, but the colour of it was like fire. And I took it, and drank: and when I had drunk of it, my heart uttered understanding, and wisdom grew in my breast, for my spirit strengthened my memory: and my mouth was opened, and shut no more. The Highest gave understanding unto the five men, and they wrote the wonderful visions of the night that were told, which they knew not: and they sat forty days, and they wrote in the day, and at night they ate bread. As for me, I spake in the day, and I held not my tongue by night. In forty days they wrote two hundred and four books.

And it came to pass, when the forty days were fulfilled, that the Highest spake, saying, The first that thou hast written publish openly, that the worthy

The Penalty of Sin

and unworthy may read it: but keep the seventy last, that thou mayest deliver them only to such as be wise among the people: for in them is the spring of understanding, the fountain of wisdom, and the stream of knowledge. And I did so.

* Behold, speak thou in the ears of my people the words of prophecy, which I will put in thy mouth, saith the Lord: and cause them to be written in paper: for they are faithful and true. Fear not the imaginations against thee, let not the incredulity of them trouble thee, that speak against thee. For all the unfaithful shall die in their unfaithfulness.

Behold, saith the Lord, I will bring plagues upon the world; the sword, famine, death, and destruction. For wickedness hath exceedingly polluted the whole earth, and their hurtful works are fulfilled. Therefore saith the Lord, I will hold my tongue no more as touching their wickedness, which they profanely commit, neither will I suffer them in those things, in which they wickedly exercise themselves: behold, the innocent and righteous blood crieth unto me, and the souls of the just complain continually. And therefore, saith the Lord, I will surely avenge them, and receive unto me all the innocent blood from among them. Behold, my people is led as a flock to the slaughter: I will not suffer them now to dwell in the land of Egypt: but I will bring them with a mighty hand and a stretched out arm, and smite

Woe to the World & its Inhabitants

Egypt with plagues, as before, and will destroy all the land thereof. Egypt shall mourn, and the foundation of it shall be smitten with the plague and punishment that God shall bring upon it. They that till the ground shall mourn: for their seeds shall fail through the blasting and hail, and with a fearful constellation. Woe to the world and them that dwell therein! For the sword and their destruction draweth nigh, and one people shall stand up to fight against another, and swords in their hands. For there shall be sedition among men, and invading one another; they shall not regard their kings nor princes, and the course of their actions shall stand in their power. A man shall desire to go into a city, and shall not be able. For because of their pride the cities shall be troubled, the houses shall be destroyed, and men shall be afraid. A man shall have no pity upon his neighbour, but shall destroy their houses with the sword, and spoil their goods, because of the lack of bread, and for great tribulation.

Behold, saith God, I will call together all the kings of the earth to reverence me, which are from the rising of the sun, from the south, from the east, and Libanus; to turn themselves one against another, and repay the things that they have done to them. Like as they do yet this day unto my chosen, so will I do also, and recompense in their bosom. Thus saith the Lord God; My right hand shall not spare the sinners, and my sword shall not cease over them

The Horrible Vision from the East

that shed innocent blood upon the earth. The fire is gone forth from his wrath, and hath consumed the foundations of the earth, and the sinners, like the straw that is kindled. Woe to them that sin, and keep not my commandments! saith the Lord. I will not spare them: go your way, ye children, from the power, defile not my sanctuary. For the Lord knoweth all them that sin against him, and therefore delivereth he them unto death and destruction. For now are the plagues come upon the whole earth, and ye shall remain in them: for God shall not deliver you, because ye have sinned against him.

Behold an horrible vision, and the appearance thereof from the east: where the nations of the dragons of Arabia shall come out with many chariots, and the multitude of them shall be carried as the wind upon earth, that all they which hear them may fear and tremble. Also the Carmanians raging in wrath shall go forth as the wild boars of the wood, and with great power shall they come, and join battle with them, and shall waste a portion of the land of the Assyrians. And then shall the dragons have the upper hand, remembering their nature; and if they shall turn themselves, conspiring together in great power to persecute them, then these shall be troubled, and keep silence through their power, and shall flee. And from the land of the Assyrians shall the enemy besiege them, and consume some of them, and in their host shall be fear and dread, and strife

The Horrible Vision from the East

among their kings. Behold clouds from the east and from the north unto the south, and they are very horrible to look upon, full of wrath and storm. They shall smite one upon another, and they shall smite down a great multitude of stars upon the earth, even their own star; and blood shall be from the sword unto the belly, and dung of men unto the camel's hough. And there shall be great fearfulness and trembling upon earth: and they that see the wrath shall be afraid, and trembling shall come upon them. And then shall there come great storms from the south, and from the north, and another part from the west. And strong winds shall arise from the east, and shall open it; and the cloud which he raised up in wrath, and the star stirred to cause fear toward the east and west wind, shall be destroyed. The great and mighty clouds shall be lifted up full of wrath, and the star, that they may make all the earth afraid, and them that dwell therein; and they shall pour out over every high and eminent place an horrible star, fire, and hail, and flying swords, and many waters, that all fields may be full, and all rivers, with the abundance of great waters. And they shall break down the cities and walls, mountains and hills, trees of the wood, and grass of the meadows, and their corn. And they shall go stedfastly unto Babylon, and make her afraid. They shall come to her, and besiege her, the star and all wrath shall they pour out upon her: then shall the dust and smoke go

The Recompense of Asia

up unto the heaven, and all they that be about her shall bewail her.

And they that remain under her shall do service unto them that have put her in fear. And thou, Asia, that art partaker of the hope of Babylon, and art the glory of her person: woe be unto thee, thou wretch, because thou hast made thyself like unto her; and hast decked thy daughters in whoredom, that they might please and glory in thy lovers, which have alway desired to commit whoredom with thee! Thou hast followed her that is hated in all her works and inventions: therefore saith God, I will send plagues upon thee; widowhood, poverty, famine, sword, and pestilence, to waste thy houses with destruction and death. And the glory of thy power shall be dried up as a flower, when the heat shall arise that is sent over thee. Thou shalt be weakened as a poor woman with stripes, and as one chastised with wounds, so that the mighty and lovers shall not be able to receive thee. Would I with jealousy have so proceeded against thee, saith the Lord. If thou hadst not always slain my chosen, exalting the stroke of thine hands, and saying over their dead, when thou wast drunken, Set forth the beauty of thy countenance? The reward of thy whoredom shall be in thy bosom, therefore shalt thou receive recompence. Like as thou hast done unto my chosen, saith the Lord, even so shall God do unto thee, and shall deliver thee into mischief. Thy children shall die of hunger, and

Woe to Babylon, Asia, Egypt & Syria

thou shalt fall through the sword: thy cities shall be broken down, and all thine shall perish with the sword in the field. They that be in the mountains shall die of hunger, and eat their own flesh, and drink their own blood, for very hunger of bread, and thirst of water. Thou as unhappy shalt come through the sea, and receive plagues again. And in the passage they shall rush on the idle city, and shall destroy some portion of thy land, and consume part of thy glory, and shall return to Babylon that was destroyed. And thou shalt be cast down by them as stubble, and they shall be unto thee as fire; and shall consume thee, and thy cities, thy land, and thy mountains; all thy woods and thy fruitful trees shall they burn up with fire. Thy children shall they carry away captive, and, look, what thou hast, they shall spoil it, and mar the beauty of thy face.

* Woe be unto thee, Babylon, and Asia! woe be unto thee, Egypt, and Syria! Gird up yourselves with cloths of sack and hair, bewail your children, and be sorry; for your destruction is at hand. A sword is sent upon you, and who may turn it back? A fire is sent among you, and who may quench it? Plagues are sent unto you, and what is he that may drive them away? May any man drive away an hungry lion in the wood? or may any one quench the fire in stubble, when it hath begun to burn? May one turn again the arrow that is shot of a strong archer?

The mighty Lord sendeth the plagues, and who is

The Anger of the Lord revealed

he that can drive them away? A fire shall go forth from his wrath, and who is he that may quench it? He shall cast lightnings, and who shall not fear? He shall thunder, and who shall not be afraid? The Lord shall threaten, and who shall not be utterly beaten to powder at his presence? The earth quaketh, and the foundations thereof; the sea ariseth up with waves from the deep, and the waves of it are troubled, and the fishes thereof also, before the Lord, and before the glory of his power: for strong is his right hand that bendeth the bow, his arrows that he shooteth are sharp, and shall not miss, when they begin to be shot into the ends of the world.

Behold, the plagues are sent, and shall not return again, until they come upon the earth. The fire is kindled, and shall not be put out, till it consume the foundation of the earth. Like as an arrow which is shot of a mighty archer returneth not backward: even so the plagues that shall be sent upon earth shall not return again. Woe is me! woe is me! who will deliver me in those days?

The beginning of sorrows and great mournings; the beginning of famine and great death; the beginning of wars, and the powers shall stand in fear; the beginning of evils! what shall I do when these evils shall come? Behold, famine and plague, tribulation and anguish, are sent as scourges for amendment. But for all these things they shall not turn from their wickedness, nor be alway mindful of the scourges.

The Evils to come

Behold, victuals shall be so good cheap upon earth, that they shall think themselves to be in good case, and even then shall evils grow upon earth, sword, famine, and great confusion. For many of them that dwell upon earth shall perish of famine; and the other, that escape the hunger, shall the sword destroy.

And the dead shall be cast out as dung, and there shall be no man to comfort them: for the earth shall be wasted, and the cities shall be cast down. There shall be no man left to till the earth, and to sow it. The trees shall give fruit, and who shall gather them? the grapes shall ripen, and who shall tread them? for all places shall be desolate of men: so that one man shall desire to see another, and to hear his voice. For of a city there shall be ten left, and two of the field, which shall hide themselves in the thick groves, and in the clefts of the rocks. As in an orchard of olives upon every tree there are left three or four olives; or as when a vineyard is gathered, there are left some clusters of them that diligently seek through the vineyard:

Even so in those days there shall be three or four left by them that search their houses with the sword. And the earth shall be laid waste, and the fields thereof shall wax old, and her ways and all her paths shall grow full of thorns, because no man shall travel therethrough. The virgins shall mourn, having no bridegrooms; the women shall mourn, having no

The Evils to come

husbands; their daughters shall mourn, having no helpers. In the wars shall their bridegrooms be destroyed, and their husbands shall perish of famine.

Hear now these things, and understand them, ye servants of the Lord. Behold the word of the Lord, receive it: believe not the gods of whom the Lord spake. Behold, the plagues draw nigh, and are not slack. As when a woman with child in the ninth month bringeth forth her son, within two or three hours of her birth great pains compass her womb, which pains, when the child cometh forth, they slack not a moment: even so shall not the plagues be slack to come upon the earth, and the world shall mourn, and sorrows shall come upon it on every side.

O my people, hear my word: make you ready to the battle, and in those evils be even as pilgrims upon the earth. He that selleth, let him be as he that fleeth away: and he that buyeth, as one that will lose: he that occupieth merchandise, as he that hath no profit by it: and he that buildeth, as he that shall not dwell therein: he that soweth, as if he should not reap: so also he that planteth the vineyard, as he that shall not gather the grapes: they that marry, as they that shall get no children; and they that marry not, as the widowers. And therefore they that labour labour in vain: for strangers shall reap their fruits, and spoil their goods, overthrow their houses, and take their children captives, for in captivity and

Righteousness shall yet reign

famine shall they get children. And they that occupy their merchandise with robbery, the more they deck their cities, their houses, their possessions, and their own persons: the more will I be angry with them for their sin, saith the Lord. Like as a whore envieth a right honest and virtuous woman: so shall righteousness hate iniquity, when she decketh herself, and shall accuse her to her face, when he cometh that shall defend him that diligently searcheth out every sin upon earth.

And therefore be ye not like thereunto, nor to the works thereof. For yet a little, and iniquity shall be taken away out of the earth, and righteousness shall reign among you. Let not the sinner say that he hath not sinned: for God shall burn coals of fire upon his head, which saith before the Lord God and his glory, I have not sinned. Behold, the Lord knoweth all the works of men, their imaginations, their thoughts, and their hearts: which spake but the word, Let the earth be made; and it was made: Let the heaven be made; and it was created. In his word were the stars made, and he knoweth the number of them. He searcheth the deep, and the treasures thereof; he hath measured the sea, and what it containeth. He hath shut the sea in the midst of the waters, and with his word hath he hanged the earth upon the waters. He spreadeth out the heavens like a vault; upon the waters hath he founded it. In the desert hath he made springs

God is Judge: fear Him

of water, and pools upon the tops of the mountains, that the floods might pour down from the high rocks to water the earth. He made man, and put his heart in the midst of the body, and gave him breath, life, and understanding. Yea, and the Spirit of Almighty God, which made all things, and searcheth out all hidden things in the secrets of the earth, surely he knoweth your inventions, and what ye think in your hearts, even them that sin, and would hide their sin.

Therefore hath the Lord exactly searched out all your works, and he will put you all to shame. And when your sins are brought forth, ye shall be ashamed before men, and your own sins shall be your accusers in that day. What will ye do? or how will ye hide your sins before God and his angels? Behold, God himself is the judge, fear him: leave off from your sins, and forget your iniquities, to meddle no more with them for ever: so shall God lead you forth, and deliver you from all trouble.

For, behold, the burning wrath of a great multitude is kindled over you, and they shall take away certain of you, and feed you, being idle, with things offered unto idols. And they that consent unto them shall be had in derision and in reproach, and trodden under foot. For there shall be in every place, and in the next cities, a great insurrection upon those that fear the Lord. They shall be like mad men, sparing none, but still spoiling and destroying those that fear

God the Guide of Israel

the Lord, for they shall waste and take away their goods, and cast them out of their houses. Then shall they be known, who are my chosen; and they shall be tried as the gold in the fire.

Hear, O ye my beloved, saith the Lord: behold, the days of trouble are at hand, but I will deliver you from the same. Be ye not afraid, neither doubt; for God is your guide, and the guide of them who keep my commandments and precepts, saith the Lord God: let not your sins weigh you down, and let not your iniquities lift up themselves. Woe be unto them that are bound with their sins, and covered with their iniquities, like as a field is covered over with bushes, and the path thereof covered with thorns, that no man may travel through! It is left undressed, and is cast unto the fire to be consumed therewith.

Notes

FIRST ESDRAS.

p. 1, l. 1-p. 7, l. 20. All this is a repetition of 2 Chron. xxxv. 1-xxxvi. 23. But in the Canonical Bible, Hebrew and English, Ezra i. 1-3*a* is the only repetition, and it is the same as 2 Chron. xxxvi. 22 f. Herein is a bit of interesting history. The Hebrew Book of Ezra is evidently the work of the same hand that wrote Chronicles. The language, style and ideas all agree to show this. Ezra was once the proper close of the Book of Chronicles. The Chronicler wrote a full and new narrative of the Jews, from the Creation, at Adam, down to his own day, some time after Jaddua, the high priest, who welcomed Alexander the Great to Jerusalem about 330 B.C., as Josephus tells us. But this new rival of the old Bible was disliked; it seemed to discredit all the books from Genesis to Kings. The latter part of the new work, however, described the affairs during the Exile, especially those under Ezra; so it was counted valuable and almost indispensable, because 2 Kings ended at Zedekiah, the last Hebrew king before the Exile, *i.e.*, about 588 B.C. Therefore these 'Ezra' chapters were torn off the original 'Chronicles,' and added to the Sacred Canonical Collection, long before the rest of Chronicles grew important enough to get in. This 'rest' was the very last book to get in. 'Ezra' stands before it in the Hebrew Bible, while 'Chronicles' is last in that collection. Possibly these 'Ezra' chapters were literally 'torn off,' or it may be that different copies were made by different copyists; of whom one seems to have begun his copying at one point, and another at another. So Ezra i. in Hebrew begins at a later point than does 1 Esdras i. in Greek.

p. 2, l. 19. Thus sacrifices were sacred meals for all the

people, and not for priests only. And the food was made tasty.

p. 2, l. 26. These are the additional ranks of Temple hierarchy, developed in Judaism, and going far beyond the three orders named in Exodus, viz., 'High Priests, Priests, and Levites.' These new orders were called collectively 'Nethinim,' *i.e.*, 'Devotees.'

p. 3, l. 13. In 2 Kings xxiii. 22 the comparison goes farther back than Samuel, viz., to the 'Judges.'

p. 4, l. 15. 'In his second chariot' is possibly a misreading of the Hebrew words for 'in his chariot dead.' *See* 2 Kings.

p. 6, l. 8. This means surely an attack on the character of the priesthood of the writer's day.

p. 6, l. 18. These Chaldeans, or more properly 'Casdim,' were in the later times a venerated class of religious officers in Babylon. Foreigners like the Jews might easily come to give the name to the whole government of Babylon.

p. 7, l. 9. The title 'king of the Persians,' used for Cyrus or for any other Persian emperor, shows that the writer lived when the Persian empire was a thing of the far past.

p. 7, l. 20. Since the middle of this verse is the same as the end of 2 Chron. xxxvi. 23, and those last words of Chronicles do not finish the sentence as it is finished properly in 1 Esdras ii. 5, we may be sure that the close of the Second Book of Chronicles was caused by a careless hand. The end, *i.e.*, the Ezra book, was apparently torn off. Perhaps the two different copyists of Ezra and Esdras had done their work first, and then, much later, when Chronicles was being copied into the Sacred Collection, the copyist stopped suddenly and carelessly because he saw he was re-writing what was already in the 'Canon' in 'Ezra.'

p. 10, l. 18. This story is far better written than the rest of the book. The style marks it as the work of a fairly-cultured Greek.

p. 12, l. 9. In the Lucian text of the Septuagint, which was the unauthorised version in Antioch and Constantinople in the fourth century, this verse has a peculiar doublet. It runs, 'It' (*i.e.*, wine) 'maketh everyone talk by the measure of talents' (or 'millions,' as we should say, perhaps); 'and it maketh everyone according to the measure of grammes.' We should put it that 'when men are in their cups, they magnify things one moment, and minimise them the next.'

p. 14, l. 26. The picture of the love-crazed king is life-like.

p. 17, l. 4. This reads like a prototype of the English faith that a man's house is his castle.

p. 18, l. 17. The student of music will probably interpret these three terms as (1) either 'songs,' or stringed instruments; (2) instruments of percussion; (3) wind instruments. Music was, thus early, developing well under Greek influence.

p. 19, l. 1. Here is the proper close of the story of the three young officers, their contest of literary wit, and Zorobabel's success.

p. 19, l. 4. Here begins again the version properly parallel to Ezra ii.

p. 19, ll. 22, 23. Many variations in the MSS. occur here.

p. 22, l. 15. 'Atharias' is a misreading of Nehemiah's old Persian title 'the Tirshasha.' *See* Ezra ii. 63, etc. The Lucian text of the LXX. writes it 'the Atarasthas.' The Greek translator took it to be a personal name, and then set 'and' between the two names.

p. 22, ll. 16, 17. The words translated 'until there arose up a high priest clothed with doctrine and truth' correspond to the words in Ezra, 'until a priest should stand for Urim and Thummim,' *i.e.*, 'for Lights and Perfections.' These expressions have both came from the ordinance in the priestly document in Exod. xxviii. 15 ff., which says that the high priest shall wear a breastplate bearing twelve flashing jewels, with which he may divine. In 1 Sam. xxviii. 6 we read how 'Saul got no Divine answers, by dreams, by Urim' (lights), 'by inspired men.' The passage is Iahwistic and very old. Out of the traditions about such methods of divination doubtless the priestly writer of the Aaronic system developed his idea of a breastplate to be used for divinations. But we see from the translator's version 'clothed with doctrine and truth' that the thought of such divination by flashing stones had gone by his time.

p. 24, l. 4. 'Carrs.' The Greek word means 'nuts' or 'pulleys.' Guthe, in Kautzsch's *Apokryphen*, puts instead 'oil.' The Hebrew in Ezra iii. 6 has 'oil.' Some mistake must have been made by a copyist long ago.

p. 24, l. 26. Two more sorts of music are named. Valuable also is the expression, 'praising according to David.' This helps us to understand how some late Maccabean Psalms in our Psalm Book were styled 'Psalm of,' or 'to,' or 'according to,' or 'for David.' Evidently a particular class of Worship-Song was commonly described as 'of' or 'to' or 'for David,' *i.e.*, it belonged to a particular sort of composition and musical accompaniment. The name of the ancient and musical monarch, or of someone bearing equally the name 'David,' *i.e.*, 'Beloved,' was used as typical of these compositions, just as we use the term 'Gregorian.'

p. 27, l. 9. This information may be of interest to architects, as it tells how two thousand years ago builders would erect such great houses by laying three 'rows' of polished stone, and then one row of woodwork, here called 'new' and 'native.' Possibly these 'rows' were 'stories.'

p. 31, l. 17. These sacrificial meals were merry occasions. Robertson Smith has shown how such was the character of all Semitic sacrifice, until dark times came, and while the troubles lasted. But men were glad to go back to the old way. '*Non timor primus deos fecit.*'

p. 31, l. 23. The word 'Ezra' is suggestive. First let us notice that the word 'Esdras' shows how a Greek could put a sibilant sound before a dental: but the Hebrew had to do the opposite. Then the word 'Ezra' is Aramaic, not Hebrew. The 'a' at the end is the article in that Aramaic language that had crept into Judah in these later times. The whole word means 'the help.' Possibly it meant at first 'the help' that was given by Babylonian descendants of the old Hebrews to their blood-relations in Judah who were building up the new Jewish religion there. And that help was very great. Then personification of the idea might arise and be followed by the abundant traditions we have concerning this 'Ezra.' 'Ezra' may really mean many men, and not exactly one. It is significant that recent scholarly works on 'Names' pass 'Ezra' by without mention.

p. 32, l. 1. This verse is an unfinished sentence in the Greek. It is long, and the writer forgot to close it duly. It runs, 'When the order of Artaxerxes reached Esdras . . . of which a copy is subjoined: "King Artaxerxes to Esdras . . . greeting! And I (Artaxerxes) having decided,"' etc., etc. But there is no apodosis to this protasis; the 'when,' etc., has no 'then,' etc., after it, as we expect.

p. 32, l. 13. This is an exaltation of the Jewish scribe or rabbi, or member of the great or long Synagogue, *i.e.*, of that succession of studious Jews who were wont to sit and talk together in order to develop the true Torah or doctrine of God.

p. 35, l. 23. This implies a startling charge against the hierarchy. We must remember that events of such sort and persons of such offices could not easily exist in Babylon at the date supposed, *i.e.*, a century and a half after the peoples and priests and princes had been carried away thither. Hebrews would hardly hold priestly offices in Babylon still, after six generations of human life there had passed away. The real history to be seen in the story is a very real one: it is that the writer in the times from 200 B.C. on to 100 A.D. distrusted the priests whom he saw about him.

p. 38, l. 48. Here is another valuable illustration of the writer's genuine and honest subjectivity. This list of 'Gentiles' could not be objectively existent either in 450 B.C., Artaxerxes' time, or at any later date. But the words express a real mental attitude of the author.

p. 39, l. 6-p. 40, l. 20. This prayer is at once fierce, fanatical, hard, cruel toward homes, loves, children, wives, and it is pathetic, and moves one to sympathy by its hunger for some—ay, any, the most costly—qualification for approach to God.

Besides, it is a touching proof of that faith in the mighty grace of God which dwells in the hardest souls, and often bursts forth from them.

p. 41, l. 25-p. 42, l. 10. The writer has indeed dramatic power! His picture of the troubled crowd, shivering under the fanatic voice, and the gloomy pouring skies, for days together, moves one's heart now after these long ages.

p. 44, l. 7. Again come picturesque touches. They are bright now as they paint for us the autumn dance feast, the synagogue pulpit, the eager reader, the interpreter or expounding preacher. Then very touching are the words about 'those who had nothing to eat' on that day when all others feasted. So we are lifted to the fine record of the tender counsel to the well-to-do, to 'send part to those hungry ones.' And these were nobly kind: they did so send! So the story ends, torn off indeed, yet at a happy point, where everybody 'made great cheer.'

N.B.—The student should study the English Revised Version of the book, the Greek in Lagarde's 'Lucian' text, and in Tischendorf's edition; also Bissell's 'Apocrypha' in Lange's *Bible Commentary;* and, in German, especially Guthe's study of the book in Kautzsch's *Apokryphen*, and Fritzsche's Notes in the *Kurzgefasstes exegetisches Handbuch* for the Apocrypha.

SECOND ESDRAS.

p. 46, l. 1. This is the prefixed Christian setting. The influence of the New Testament upon its author is evident, as we shall see by noticing particular passages. Mr James, in editing Professor Bensly's 'Text of Fourth' (*i.e.*, our Second) 'Esdras,' describes certain close affinities between these two chapters and several early Christian works, notably the so-called 'Apocalypse of Zephaniah,' recently made accessible among texts edited by Harnack. The two chapters have been pieced together with the probable purpose to adapt and convert the Apocalypse proper, following in chaps. iii.-xiv., from its original use as a Jewish book of comfort into a support for Christians.

p. 47, l. 9. The writer uses here both Exodus and also Ps. lxxviii., especially ver. 25.

p. 48, l. 8. Here is the kernel argument for the Christian in his appropriation of the work. The Jews had refused the offered blessings; therefore God had turned to bless other peoples. The Christian writer imputes this utterance to the very Esdras whom the Jewish writer had counted so utterly devoted to Judaism. The appropriator acted of course according to the method of the times, and he fully believed that 'Ezra' would have held and uttered this judgment on the Jews.

p. 48, l. 24. These beautiful words of Matt. xxiii. 37 and Luke xiii. 34, given there as our Lord's own, are now and here imputed to Esdras as a prophecy delivered by him about 400 B.C. Even such a misappropriation was quite possible by this Christian writer.

p. 48, l. 29. These words seem taken from Matt. xxiii. 34, 38, and Luke xiii. 33-35.

p. 49, l. 16. So this verse seems an echo of John xx. 29.

p. 49, l. 20. This valuation of 'the twelve' prophets ranks them very high, placing them as 'leaders' alongside of Abraham, Isaac and Jacob.

And the writer knew that the Book of 'Malachi' was perhaps not written by some one bearing that word as a personal name. He knew Hebrew and the little book, enough to see that the word means 'my servant.' Some say Ezra was Malachi!

p. 50, l. 25-p. 52, l. 25. Here are a succession of fine utterances of faith in Immortality.

p. 50, l. 27. This is clearly an echo of our Lord's words in Matt. xi. 28.

p. 52, l. 18. Esdras is credited with the same dignity as Moses; perhaps they are counted as one and the same soul.

p. 52, l. 22. The Latin Version contains in these verses the well-known words, 'Requiem æternitatis dahit vobis, quoniam in proximo est ille, qui in finem sæculi adveniet. Parati estote ad præmia regni, quia lux perpetua lucebit nobis per æternitatem temporis.' This is used in the Roman Catholic office for the dead. Hence that office and music set to it receive the name 'Requiem.'

p. 53, l. 3-p. 53, l. 9, are echoes of the Revelation of John.

p. 53, l. 9. This declaration that 'the number of the elect is fulfilled' has reference to the oracle of the First Vision (chaps. iii.-v.), which says that this number must be fulfilled before the new Age or Æon can begin. So the early Christians believed that this new age was to begin immediately. Singularly, in the Anglican 'Office for the Burial of the Dead,' the first prayer traverses this faith.

p. 53, l. 15. Our Lord Jesus appears, glorified and awarding the confessors' palms, a conception that arose amid the persecutions and martyrdoms of the second century.

p. 54, l. 6. Here begins the apocalypse proper, the real Jewish book.

p. 54, l. 6.-p. 56, l. 17. The date of the revelations to Esdras is set as 'the thirtieth year after the ruin of the city.' The only ruin of the city which occurred before 450 B.C., *i.e.*, the days of Esdras, was in 588 B.C., a century and a half before; so this is probably not intended. The thirty years must be counted from the destruction of Jerusalem by the Romans in A.D. 70. So the book was written about 100 A.D. This agrees with the conclusion drawn from the Fifth Vision (chap. xii. 28), that the writer lived under the Roman Emperor Domitian.

p. 54, l. 6. The critical text of Bensly puts instead of the pronoun 'I' the words, 'I, Salathiel, who am also Esdras.' Perhaps by using thus the name of Salathiel, who was the father of Zorobabel, and lived therefore about 550 B.C., the writer meant to set the date of the oracles as actually 558 B.C., *i.e.*, just thirty years after the first fall of Jerusalem. Then he would identify Salathiel with Ezra, making the latter an elder of great age.

p. 54, l. 13. This account of Creation follows that given in Gen. ii., the Second or Iahwistic narrative.

p. 55, l. 20. This is an echo of Ps. xviii. 9.

p. 55, l. 29. Paul's idea of a 'first Adam' or 'first mankind,' and a 'second Adam' or 'new mankind' was quite a Jewish conception.

The passage, and many like it, as we shall see, show how deeply the Jews' minds were filled with the idea of a total depravity of mankind. And the idea included still more: the total depravity was caused by original depravity implanted in Adam at his creation, and this included of course the belief in the inheritance of depravity. All this grew out of the idea of a physically holy seed, into which men were born if they were children of Abraham; or out of which men were excluded if they were not his descendants. Then this theory broke down, on one of its sides, with the rise of the moral prophets, whose preaching to a great degree overthrew the idea of 'goodness by descent.' But it only threw many Hebrews over into the 'outside sinful seed,' and made larger the number of those 'born sinners.' Certainly it was all a phase of the deepening of the moral consciousness.

p. 57, l. 11. The First Vision begins here, and is an eloquent exposition of the doctrine of the 'Incomprehensibility of Deity.'

p. 57, l. 22-p. 58, l. 24, are skilfully conceived illustrations, somewhat Socratic in method.

p. 60, l. 3. Here crosses our path the first breath of the Jewish despair over the present world, and the hope in the next alone, that will presently pervade every utterance of the seer.

p. 60, l. 20-p. 62, l. 25. The anxious study of the 'signs of the times' begins now. It absorbs the writer, as it did men of whom we read in the New Testament, as in Matt. xxiv. 3, Luke xii., and 1 and 2 Thess., and the Revelations of John.

p. 64, l. 3. This 'Salathiel' would surely be a second person of the name; we saw that the seer of the book was called 'Salathiel and also Esdras.' But Bensly's critical text gives 'Phaltiel' here instead of 'Salathiel.'

p. 64, l. 13. We reach now the Second Vision, which is greatly occupied with 'Hereafter,' but rather in an introductory way, and bidding both seer and men 'Be hopeful because there is to be a blessed future.' The devout Jews were driven by their sorrows to despair concerning the present Life or Æon. This Second Vision is the first answer of comfort. Another answer will follow in the Third Vision.

p. 65, l. 15-p. 66, l. 14, are fine conceptions of the great love of God, as far beyond human loves. We shall find this idea repeated often.

p. 65, l. 19. Here is an expression, 'part of His judgment,' which has resulted from a misinterpretation of the Hebrew of the original. The original Hebrew words could easily be misread thus, but they meant 'His decision at the Judgment.' Wellhausen and Gunkel have disclosed a number of these mistakes, all being signs that the original book was written in Hebrew.

p. 65, l. 19-p. 66, l. 25. These utterances reveal a very agony of soul in the writer, as he wrestled with God for understanding.

p. 68, l. 23. The cry bursts out again, 'When shall this weary age end?'

p. 71, l. 7. The Third Vision begins here. It is perhaps the loftiest of all the Seven. While the First had cried, amid mystery, 'God knows more than we,' and the Second said, 'Let us hope for a Hereafter,' now this Third describes the blisses and the woes in that Future.

p. 75, l. 6. 'There is no Judge above God.' This may be a polemic against early Christian conceptions concerning Jesus and His followers.

p. 75, l. 27. The word 'Jesus' may have been inserted by a Christian copyist, instead of 'Christ,' which itself occurs hard by. Yet the conception and name and offices of 'Jesus,' *i.e.*, 'God's Saviour,' were thoroughly of Jewish origin. The word 'Ieshu' was familiar to the Pharisee lovers and writers of Psalms.

p. 75, l. 27 ff. And now begins exposition of the Jewish doctrine of 'The Anointed.' It is not right to use the word 'Messiah' for this; for that word has a doubled second consonant, which makes it signify 'one *constantly* and *utterly* anointed,' and this word occurs only in the New Testament. The word commonly used in the Old Testament for a king, *e.g.*, for David, or for Cyrus, or for a priest, was 'Masiah,' *i.e.*, 'One who is once anointed.' The early Christians evidently coined the stronger word. The Greek word 'Christ' is set equally for both words. The Greek speech and mind could not appreciate the Hebrew reverence for this new sort of *Messiah*, our Lord Jesus. The Jewish 'Anointed One' was to be a 'Son of God.' His reign was to last 400 years. Then He would die and remain so for seven years, and rise again with all souls.

p. 76, l. 3. During this week of years all things were to be silent and dead awaiting the great and general Resurrection, after which would come the 'Day of Judgment.'

p. 76, l. 14. After this verse follow the seventy verses that were lost, from the current Latin Version, for nearly a thousand years. Professor Gildemeister's description of the MS. from which all those copies were made is exceedingly interesting. He is quoted in Bensly's 'Missing Fragment,' p. 5, thus, 'On collating the Codex of St. Germains I discovered that the missing passage between vii. 35 and 36 was once contained therein. . . . A leaf which originally came between these verses has been cut out, leaving about half an inch of its inner margin.' And Professor Bensly describes on p. 9 what he saw himself thus, 'A slight inspection sufficed to show the correctness of Professor Gildemeister's statement with regard to the excision of a leaf . . . there are only seven leaves . . . the third has no fellow, for the sixth has been cut out with a knife, traces of which have been left on the fifth.'

Professor Bensly's account of his discovery of a Latin MS. at Amiens, which does contain the missing passage, is excellent, 'An article in the catalogue . . . of Amiens . . . caught my eye. . . . The perusal of a few verses . . . of the MS. served to show the great value of this new critical aid. I read on . . . approached the place of . . . chasm . . . my eyes glided on to the words "et apparebit . . ." I knew that the oldest and best translation of this passage was at last recovered.'

The English Revised Version of the Apocrypha numbers the restored verses thus [36], [37], etc.

p. 83, l. 25. This in Revised Version is of course ver. [105] 36.

p. 84, l. 24. [48], [63], [68] and 118 [48] are sad utterances of the belief in created, inborn, original sin. The writer is not talking of others, but means himself. As Professor Gunkel says, he is truly tender, as all Judaism of this troubled time was tenderly disposed because bowed down with sorrow. And he is far too manly to weaken or blunt the point and home-thrust of his arguments. 'He has a torn heart, a soul heavy-laden with tormenting thoughts, im Kampf um die Weltanschauung.' 'The book is the most sympathetic among all the apocalypses.'

p. 77, l. 11. Again the 'week of years' of the Intermediate state.

p. 80, l. 6. Here is an inquiry whether in the Intermediate state the dead rest or are tormented.

p. 80, l. 25 ff. Dante-like cycles: seven torments and seven orders of joy.

p. 86, l. 24. This is somewhat like Matt. xx. 16 and xxii. 14; but rather is it exactly the same, in words and fear, as the cry of the Jewish questioner of Luke xiii. 23, who begged our Lord for light concerning this gloomy, if conscientious, Jewish doctrine.

p. 88, l. 5 ff. From this point to ver. 36 is a prayer, which is contained also separately in the Canticles of the Vulgate. It is known as the 'Confession of Esdras.' The original Latin version of it has been displaced from the current texts by that which we usually read, which is considerably different from the other, and bears the title which forms the latter part of ver. 19.

p. 88, l. 17. Another Latin misreading of the original Hebrew. The Hebrew meant, 'Whose truth standeth for ever.' Our faulty version is, 'Which the truth witnesseth.' The Hebrew words meaning 'for ever' and 'witness' are very much alike. Hence the mistake.

p. 90, l. 20. Again 'God's love is far, far greater than human loves.'

p. 91, l. 3. The writer tries to grasp a hope of salvation for himself: he counts himself perhaps to be 'saved, yet so as by fire.'

p. 91, l. 22. The idea of a Day of Judgment was thoroughly Jewish. The Hebrew Amos had used it; Zephaniah also.

p. 92, ll. 1-8. This is much like Matt. xxiv. 1-11, which is a very Jewish passage dating from about the same time as our booklet.

p. 92, l. 15. The doctrine of Salvation b Works was Jewish; and Paul fought against, while James stoodyfor it.

p. 92, l. 23. Not unlike the allegory of Lazarus and the rich man, another Jewish conception, which lets the good Jew rest in Abraham's bosom in the Hereafter.

p. 93, l. 29. A curious way of preparation for inspiration by living in the fields and eating only flowers and herbs. This is like John's way of life.

p. 94, l. 5. The Fourth Vision begins here. This and the Fifth and Sixth are dreams and extravagant, while the former three were studious dialogues. This fourth expounds a doctrine of Zion as Mother of the best children, who perish sadly just on the threshold of bliss. Esdras, like the true prophet of Isa. xl., seeks tenderly to comfort her. The interpretation seems unfinished. We wish to know whether the glistening beauty of ix. 26 ff. signified coming glory.

p. 101, l. 8. The Fifth Vision is based on Dan. vii., and very extravagant and hard to interpret.

p. 106, l. 20-p. 107, l. 5. The date of the writer may be made out from considering the last events which the vision describes as going on. They seem to be in the reign of Domitian.

p. 107, l. 14. A foreshadowing of the doctrine of God's Anointed.

p. 107, l. 25. The hidden things of God could be grasped by certain persons like Esdras, who then might hand them on to the wise. Judaism did certainly not believe in a closed, limited, unalterable, infallible Canon. And early Christianity accepted this liberal doctrine, and held it until the iron heathenism of Roman law demanded and canonised a firmly defined statute book.

p. 109, l. 6. The doctrine of God's Anointed is now set forth by a dream in the Sixth Vision. This Jewish Christ was to be God's Son, sent as a man from the hidden Bosom, to be a DELIVERER, a 'Jesus'; but also to reprove, rebuke, correct and destroy His enemies; and to deliver His own.

p. 109, l. 29-p. 112, l. 21. His mouth, lips, tongue, *i.e.*, His teaching, make His sole weapon: but it burns up the enemies, as Malachi had taught.

p. 110, l. 13. The 'offered up' are doubtless those described in Isa. lxvi. 20 and xlix. 22 as Jewish slaves who are set free and brought by their old masters. The Epistle to the Romans uses the same idea in chap. xv. 16.

p. 111, l. 12. This faith is opposed by Paul in 1 Thess. iv. 15 ff. It troubled the early Christians. Our little book throws many a sidelight on New Testament words and ways.

p. 111, l. 16. 'Which by his own self shall deliver.' This is another misreading of Hebrew words, which mean, 'By whom He shall deliver.' The real meaning is far the finer.

p. 114, l. 12. The Seventh Vision, or Setting of the Theory of the Restoration of the Sacred Books, is full of interest and of value for the student of the development of doctrine concerning Scriptures. *See* the Introduction *supra.*

p. 115, l. 4. This system of chronology makes the present Æon or World consist of twelve parts, probably alluding to the 'twelve' tribes, or, better, to the 'twelve moons' in a year, and 'twelve signs' of the Zodiac. Of the twelve there have already passed away ten and a half, *i.e.*, by the year A.D. 100. The Jewish reckoning of *to-day* sets the Creation in the year 3760 B.C., so that by A.D. 100 ten and a half cycles of 320 years each had passed, and so our writer expected the end of the present world about 580 A.D. But below, ver. 48, sets Esdras's translation in A.M. 5000: so the end would be later still.

p. 115, l. 28. The Holy Ghost was, of course, quite as much a fact in the Jewish religion as in the Christian. He was the fountain of all inspirations, and His operation was often described, in the Hebrew literature, as by the writer of Isa. xi.

# of Esdras

p. 116, l. 10. The candle, or lamp, is not meant in a literal and material sense. By Hebrew syntax the following word 'understanding' is the defining word. The writer meant 'the lamp or light which consists in *understanding*.'

p. 117, l. 13. This 'cup' and 'draught' give a more material expression, added possibly for the sake of simpler folk. It is like Ezekiel's eaten roll, yet much less material than that. Ezekiel wishes to have the actual written document and prescriptions to eat. Our writer is beyond that.

p. 117, l. 25. The variant number '904' is a misreading of the original Latin word '*nonaginta*,' no doubt: as four chief Oriental versions have 'ninety.' Some exaggerating Latin copyist made the easy alteration into '*nongenti*.'

p. 118, l. 5. After this we find, in the Oriental versions, two and a half more verses. The three verses 48 to 50 should run: '(48) So I did in the seventh year of the sixth week—5000 years, 3 months, 12 days, after the creation of the world; (49) then Ezra was translated and taken up to the abode of his fellows, after he had written all. (50) He is called the Writer of the Knowledge of the Highest unto Everlasting.'

p. 118, l. 6. Mr James, in Bensly's text, describes these well as an imitation of the prophetical invectives of the Old Testament, written purposely as an appendix to the book, with the author's personality well held in the background. The date 268 A.D. is generally assigned to it; and it seems to allude to the wars of the Sassanide kings of Parthia against Rome and Palmyra at that time.

p. 120, l, 18. 'Carmanians' means, say some, the people of a land Kerman, now Kirman, on the Persian Gulf. Some MSS. say 'Armenians,' and that would be simple to understand. But Mr James, in Bensly's text, thinks that the old Spanish city of Carmona had to do with the word. It lies in the heart of Seville, near the home of some of the Spanish MSS.

p. 125, ll. 8-14. This has echoes of Isaiah's 'Chant of Woes,' in his chap. v. 8, etc.

p. 125, l. 18. Echoes of Isa. xvii. 5 f.

p. 127, l. 12. The eschatology here has a fine Puritan tone.

p. 127, l. 14. This uses Rom. xii. 20 singularly in its appeal to conscience.

p. 128, l. 16. Salvation by works was, of course, a feature of the Christianity that was succumbing under Jewish, and especially also Roman, traditions.

N.B.—The student should read the English Revised Version, also Dr. Bissell's. He should especially study James's edition of Bensly's text, and will be delighted with Bensly's own 'Missing Fragment,' with its photographic *facsimile* of a page of the Amiens MS. Then, above all, inspiring, elevating in all thoughtful directions, as well as full of sound information, is Professor Gunkel's treatise and translation in Kautzsch's *Pseudepigrapha*.

Colston & Coy. Limited, Printers, Edinburgh.

* 9 7 8 1 3 3 1 0 6 4 4 4 2 *

BV - #0023 - 301121 - C0 - 229/152/11 - PB - 9781331064442 - Gloss Lamination